Suffering in the World

Who's Responsible, God or Humanity?

Augustin Kassa, S.M.A.

ISBN 978-1-64492-581-2 (paperback)
ISBN 978-1-64492-582-9 (digital)

Christian Faith Publishing, Inc.
832 Park Avenue
Meadville, PA 16335
www.christianfaithpublishing.com

Imprimatur:
F.Sognon, S.M.A.
Superior of the Society of African Missions
District-in-Formation of the Gulf of Guinea, October 10, 2018

Printed in the United States of America

To the suffering members of the body of Christ

Contents

Acknowledgments

I thank God for the gift of life he granted me through my parents and family members. Profound gratitude to all my teachers and formators and friends.

A sincere thank-you to my religious order, the Society of African Missions (SMA).

Thanks to the Catholic Communities of the Ottawa Vicariate. I am grateful to all the clergy of the Diocese of Peoria, most especially to those in Ottawa Vicariate. God bless!

Introduction

In May 2011, I was ordained a deacon in Nairobi, Kenya. After the ordination, I still had two more semesters of class work before my priestly ordination. As I continued with my classes, I also did some pastoral activities at a parish in Nairobi. Part of the requirement for the priestly ordination of a transitional deacon is six months of pastoral work. Since it would have been impossible to do that after the end of the academic year due to the dates of the priestly ordination, I had to fulfill the pastoral requirement alongside my studies. I was therefore appointed, by my formation superior, to the Mary Mother of God Parish located in the diocese of Ngong in Kenya. In 2011, I would have described the parish as situated in a semi-urban area, even though life in Embulbul was a little bit more complex than can be adequately captured by such a generalized description.

One, perhaps, of the most fundamental elements of the Society of African Missions' (SMA) charism, of which I am a member, is the proclamation of the Word of God to the most abandoned people of Africa, or of African origin. It was in response to this vocation that a former SMA priest—Kevin McGarry (now married)—in 1997 started to build the parish of Embulbul that finally got inaugurated in 2003. As a parish, Embulbul was comprised of a mixed population. That is, some parishioners lived in abject poverty; others were what could be considered as belonging to the middle class, while a few of them were rich.

I first preached a sermon on the subject of suffering in the parish of Mary Mother of God in Embulbul. I remember that it was on a Good Friday. I had prepared my sermons for the *Triduum* a week prior to going to the parish for Easter celebrations. The morning of Good Friday, I went with the parochial vicar (Fr. Con Murphy, SMA) to visit an old lady who had had throat surgery. The woman lived in terrible conditions. The house where she lived was a one-room shack constructed with corrugated iron sheets. It was extremely cold, and her health was very fragile. She couldn't even afford the Ksh 20 (equivalent to 20 cents) medicated liquid that she had been advised by the doctor to drink twice a day. I was shaken from seeing the abject poverty in which the woman lived together with her children and grandchildren. By the time we returned to the rectory, I had already made up my mind. I needed to change my Good Friday sermon. I will preach about suffering, I told myself. My intention was to try and bring some consolation to the many parishioners whom I knew lived in conditions similar to the woman we just met.

I remember preparing and preaching on suffering. The title of my sermon was, "Why Suffering?" While using the language of permissibility or allowance, which I did not understand much at the time, I suggested five different points of reflection: (1) God allows suffering as a means to cure us or to discipline us. (2) God allows suffering as a way to change our hearts. (3) God allows suffering as a way to make us understand that in our lives, we must always rely on him and his grace. (4) God allows the suffering of some, for the well-being, faith, and salvation of others. And finally, (5) God allows suffering to test our faith. I then concluded my sermon with Job 19: 25, suggesting that if we hold on to God, the future will be bright. At the end of a lengthy sermon, and the long Good Friday service, I was shocked by the diversity in people's reactions. I will broadly categorize the responses into three different groups. The less fortunate of the community, the poor, perceived my sermon to be encouraging. They understood that God *allowed* them to suffer for a purpose. However, if they hold on to God their Redeemer (Job 19: 25), the future will be bright. This particular group came thanking me for my thoughtful reflection.

Others at the end of the celebration came asking, "Doesn't God know us, doesn't he know that we are already suffering? Or how long do we need to suffer for him to stop testing, and disciplining, or stop using us for the well-being of others?" And the last group found it very ridiculous, incongruous, that God does permit suffering. "If God permits suffering," they asked, "why pray?" What is the purpose of God if he cannot defend us from suffering and pain?

While the reaction of the first group was consoling, I found myself battling with the questions posed by others, for they were legitimate. Then I started to wonder if my sermon was truly helpful to the less privileged of Embulbul. Did my sermon numb them to the reality of suffering and lead them to remain resigned to their fate? How is that helpful in their lives? Aren't they supposed to continue striving for the betterment of their lives? These are just some of the multiple questions that stayed with me. Seven years after preaching that initial sermon on suffering, the reality of people who suffer around me (my mother included) has grown exponentially, I haven't been able to find a meaningful explanation to the mystery of suffering. Last summer (2007), as I took a class entitled "God and the Mystery of Human Suffering," I found Schillebeeckx's approach to suffering very interesting. His forceful insistence that God is not responsible for the death of his Son and consequently is not responsible for the suffering of humanity made a lot of sense to me. I wished I could go back and re-preach again to the poor people of Embulbul and tell them that God is not responsible for their troubles. And that greed and corrupt humanity, encouraged by the devil, is the problem there is.

Marthe Robin has remained one of my favorite mystics. My family has a longstanding tradition of asking for the intercession of Marthe. In fact, in 1989, one of my brothers, through her intercession, was saved from the well in which he fell when he was only six years old. The Foyer de Charité in Togo, my home country, is one of the first founded through the direct instruction of Marthe Robin to Fr. Léon Marcel. As a teenager, every year, we went to the Foyer de Charité in Alédjo for retreats. This is a practice that I have maintained and continued whenever I'm home on vacation.

Of the life of Marthe Robin, one thing that anyone who has ever heard of her knows is that she was a stigmatic who suffered a lot and lived fifty to fifty-one years solely on Holy Communion. While Schillebeeckx's theology of suffering made a lot of sense to me, I couldn't help but think about the case of Marthe Robin. If God is indeed not responsible for the suffering of humanity, I asked myself, then what do I make of the experience of Marthe Robin? For she maintained that her stigmata, a cause of great suffering for her, were received from Jesus.

Consequently, I started to wonder: was I right six years prior when I blindly suggested that God allows or permits suffering? Or perhaps, he is the author of pain and suffering? Or who knows, maybe God is not the cause of evil. Whatever the case, perhaps, I wished to ask: where is God when people experience suffering? Or simply, what should our response be in the face of suffering?

I will attempt in the next chapters to explore the multiple understandings and reactions of humanity to pain and suffering. I will begin by focusing my attention on the biblical tradition. What does the Bible say about suffering, its origin, and human response when faced by it? In the second chapter, I will try to discuss St. Augustine's and Thomas Aquinas' efforts to explain the origin of suffering and pain. I will peculiarly zoom in on their two evils theories and explore the meaning they give to the death of Jesus Christ. The third chapter will concentrate on the medieval perception of pain and suffering. Most importantly, I will examine how Christianity embraced suffering and pain as a way of identifying with the suffering Lord. In the fourth chapter, I will focus my attention on Schillebeeckx. The main purpose will be to highlight Schillebeeckx's conviction that suffering has no foundation whatsoever in God. To use his words, the cross (suffering) is the index of the anti-divine. The fifth chapter will be dedicated to Marthe Robin, a French mystic and contemporary of Schillebeeckx. Through her suffering, Marthe believed she was made a victim of God to show the Lord's love to the world. With the stigmata she claimed she received from God and her weekly passions, she believed herself to be united to Jesus and prayed that her suffering served the salvation of souls. I will then conclude by engaging Marthe Robin and Edward Schillebeeckx in a conversation in the final chapter which I shall entitle "The Paradox of the Cross." In that chapter, I will raise the questions related to Marthe's understanding that the cross (pain and suffering from the stigmata) is from God and how and where, if any, that intersects with Schillebeeckx's theology of God not being the author of human suffering.

Chapter 1

What Does the Bible Say about God and Suffering?

F rom time immemorial, humanity has always had to face the reality of pain and suffering. One would presume that it would be easy to just accept it as part of life. But the pinch of suffering is so painful that humankind consistently tries to trace its origin and make meaning of its existence. The attempt to understand the source or cause of suffering is motivated by our desire to avoid, to control, or perhaps just to better comprehend it. Nonetheless, not being able to stop suffering leaves human beings with multiple queries: Is suffering the result of our wrong choices, of our sinfulness, of God's judgment and punishment? What about the suffering of the innocent, the abundance of pain and suffering in the world? Above all, the untamable nature of suffering poses a dilemma about the place of God in the history of human suffering (is God at the source, in the middle, in the end, or against suffering?). How can one begin to speak of God in the face of the abysmal history of suffering in the world, in his (God's) world?[1] And ultimately, what does the Word teach us?

---

[1] Cf. Johann Baptist Metz, "Suffering unto God," trans. J. Matthew Ashley, Critical Inquiry 20, no. 4 (1994): 611–22. http://www.jstor.org/stable/1343852, 612.

1.1 *The Place of God in Suffering: A Pastoral Landscape*

First, a small detour in the pastoral world may help put my inquiry into perspective. For many years, the mystery of suffering has been explained with direct reference to God. For instance, Daniel P. Foley in "Eleven Interpretations of Personal Suffering" describes eleven different ways—of which seven make direct reference to God—through which people interpret and understand the suffering they go through. He explains that some sufferers see suffering (1) as a punishment from God;[2] (2) others, as a test of loyalty from God;[3] (3) or an opportunity for growth from God;[4] (4) still some as part of the will of God;[5] (5) or as God's way of saving one from a forthcoming worse situation;[6] (6) while others still simply take it as something that God has a meaning, a reason for;[7] (7) or again as an opportunity to join in Christ's suffering for the salvation of humanity.[8] These undeviating references to God are a reflection of how people, especially those who are religious, make recourse to God when faced with suffering. Some few examples may here help exemplify my point.

At the beginning of his book *God and the Mystery of Human Suffering: A Theological Conversation Across the Ages,* Robin Ryan presents the story of a couple (Mary and John) who, during a presentation he gave in a parish on "Prayer in Times of Suffering," shared a real-life experience. He writes,

> Mary told the group gathered [...] that about six
> months earlier her husband had been in a serious

---

[2] Daniel Patrick Foley, "Eleven Interpretations of Personal Suffering." Journal of Religion and Health 27, no. 4 (1988): 321–28. http://www.jstor.org/stable/27505991, 322.

[3] Daniel Patrick Foley, "Eleven Interpretations of Personal Suffering." 322.

[4] Ibid, 325.

[5] Ibid, 324.

[6] Ibid, 326.

[7] Ibid, 326.

[8] Ibid, 327.

automobile accident. It had occurred at night on a dark, winding road. Another car, approaching from the opposite direction and traveling at high speed, had slammed into John's car. The other car had crossed over unto the wrong side of the road. The driver of the other car was injured in the collision, though he survived the accident. John's car was damaged beyond repair, but he walked away from the crash with a few minor scratches and bruises. The state trooper who arrived first on the scene expressed his astonishment that John had not been injured more severely. The trooper said that in all his years on the police force he had never seen anything like it; he called it a "miracle." In the months subsequent to the accident Mary and John, people of strong faith, told family and friends about what had happened and expressed their sincere gratitude to God for God's providential care in the terrifying accident. They publicly praised God for John's escape from injury. Mary explained that about three months after the accident, the daughter of close friends was killed in an automobile accident. This young woman was a teenager. John and Mary reached out to their friends to walk with them through this devastating experience. Mary explained that [...] while she and John were still grateful to God for John's escape, from injury, they no longer felt comfortable talking about his deliverance in terms of "God's protection" or "divine providence." If they continued to proclaim their gratitude for God's providential care in John's life, what would their friends think? Would they conclude that God had not been exercising providential care for their teenage daughter? Were they and their daughter not as worthy of God's protection as John and Mary had been? Were they undeserving of a "miracle"?[9]

Within three months, we have two similarly life-threatening experiences with different outcomes. How do we explain the intervention of God in such circumstances? Why would God allow the death of a young teenager and save an older man? How do the biblical inferences of an all-powerful and good creator, God, and savior apply in both situations?

In January 2015, Pope Francis visited Manila, Philippines. During his visit, he encountered a young girl "tearfully recounting a young life as yet spent forced to forage for food from garbage and to sleep outside on cardboard mats, 12-year-old Glyzelle Palomar had a simple but profound question for Pope Francis. 'Why did God let this happen to us?' the young Filipino asked, covering her face with her hands as she sobbed."[10] While the reply of Pope Francis may not be of interest here, the question by the twelve-year-old girl is, for it reflects a search for the explanation of the origin and meaning of her suffering. She implies that God has power over her suffering and, in addition, allows it to happen. Similar situations have characterized my own pastoral experience; people who experience suffering always tend to bring God into their situations of pain. What did I do to God? they ask. Why is God punishing me? Why isn't God acting to save me? I ask with all these people, "Where is God in suffering—at its source, indifferent to it, or against it?"

1.2 The Scriptural Approach to Human Suffering

The Bible contains multiple approaches to the reality of suffering. In fact, Daniel Harrington suggests, "One theme that runs through the various books of the Bible is suffering—a theme that

---

[9]   Robin Ryan, God and the Mystery of Human Suffering: A Theological Conversation across the Ages (NY: Paulist Press, 2011), 1–2.

[10] Joshua J. McElwee, "Francis Struggles to Answer Crying Girl's Question about Suffering," https://www.ncronline.org/news/world/francis-struggles-an-swer-crying-girls-question-about-suffering, accessed 01/22/2018.

naturally evokes questions about the existence and nature of God, the human condition, ethics, justice, evil, sin, rewards and punishments, and life after death."[11] And since suffering and pain is experienced differently by different people in different circumstances and times, it is not difficult to understand the panoply of approaches that we find in the scriptures.

1.2.1 Lament

Suffering and pain can sometimes be overwhelming. And to deal with suffering, some Old Testament writers suggested coping with it by plaintive cries addressed to the God of the covenant. Daniel Harrington explains that the word "cope" does not mean passive acceptance of the suffering that one goes through. Rather, it is an expression of lament as articulated in some of the Psalms of the Old Testament (Psalm 3, Psalm 13, Psalm 22, etc.), where the psalmist addressed God actively and boldly.[12] The plea of the psalmist always comes after he has deplored the lamentable condition of an individual or the entire nation.[13] "In some cases, God is criticized as the cause of the suffering; in other cases, God is reminded that God's own reputation and honor are at risk."[14] While it remains true that in the Psalms of Lament, the sufferer seems to suggest that God has abandoned him or the entire nation, he knows that by appealing to and reminding him (God) of his previous care for his nation, deliverance will come. But it seems that the condition, if any, for God's intervention is the ability of the sufferer to face the reality of suffering and articulate his own questions: "Why am I suffering?" "Where is God?" "Why isn't God doing something for me?" "Why are 'they' [my enemies] allowed to triumph over me and God?"[15] The aptness of facing reality and intelligibly asking appropriate questions is the

---

[11] Daniel J. Harrington, Why Do We Suffer? A Scriptural Approach to the Human Condition (Franklin, Wis.: Sheed & Ward, 2000), viii.

[12] Cf. Daniel J. Harrington, Why Do We Suffer? 3.

[13] Cf. Daniel J. Harrington, Why Do We Suffer? 3.

[14] Ibid.

[15] Ibid, 6.

breakthrough that is needed in (1) evaluating self and embarking on conversion if need be (see Psalms 3 and 13); (2) or simply recognizing that s/he suffers because s/he "belongs to a tradition of suffering and a community of sufferers."[16] For the psalmist, whether suffering is the result of sin or merely the implication of our human nature or heritage, the only way out is God's intervention in reversing what he possibly caused or allowed (see Psalm 22).[17]

1.2.2 The Law of Retribution

Retribution is undoubtedly the loudest and the most known theology of suffering in the scriptures. Daniel Harrington concurs when he proposes that one prominent biblical answer to our questions about the cause of suffering is the law of retribution. That is, the just are rewarded, and the wicked are punished.[18] "The Pentateuch and the Historical Books use it [the theology of retribution] as a key to interpreting the history of Israel from Abraham to the exile of 587 BC. The great prophets built on it as they warned and challenged the people of God to repent."[19]

1.2.2.1 Retribution in Wisdom Literature

While there is a general understanding of the theology of retribution that runs through the Bible, it took different variations in its (Bible's) multiple books. In the books of wisdom, retribution revolved around human behavior and attitude. Ethical behavior is positively rewarded in the here and now, while bad conduct is punished with pain, suffering, and death in this present life.

> It is generally true, according to wisdom teachers, that wise and righteous behavior brings happiness, while foolish and evil conduct bring unhap-

---

[16] Ibid.
[17] Ibid, 11.
[18] Ibid, 16.
[19] Ibid.

piness, suffering, and death. In Israelite wisdom, the intellectual (wise/fools) and the moral (righteous/unrighteous) dimensions go together. Since there is little or no concept of an afterlife, the rewards and punishments are understood to apply to one's life on earth.[20]

Much more significant in the wisdom literature is the implication that people suffer the consequences of their own actions, the consequences of their own wrong choices. In Proverbs 11:3, 5, the wisdom writer states, "The integrity of the upright guides them, but the crookedness of the treacherous destroys them. The righteousness of the blameless keeps their ways straight, but the wicked fall by their own wickedness." Commenting on these passages, Daniel Harrington clearly explicates, "With such a teaching there is always the temptation to reverse the sequence. That is, one is tempted to assume that those who end up in disaster must have been both foolish and wicked."[21] A wisdom teacher also worthy of mention is Ben Sira who "accepted as true the basic assumptions that righteous and wise behavior leads to happiness, and unrighteous and foolish behavior leads to unhappiness."[22]

The second trend of retribution in wisdom literature suggests that suffering is always present. Its presence in the world is not dependent on human activities. But then, the righteous are saved from its troubles while the wicked are left to face its reality. In this context, the wisdom teacher or writer tends to maintain that the reality of pain and suffering is part of the world, but for those who are good and righteous, God grants deliverance. The evildoer, however, ends up in the midst of suffering (see Proverbs 11:8). "While 'troubles' or distress may be part of everyone's life the righteous person will either avoid it entirely or be easily extracted from it, while the wicked person falls into it ever more deeply and ends up being destroyed

---

[20] Ibid, 17.
[21] Ibid, 18.
[22] Ibid, 20.

by it."[23] The author of the book of the Sirach, Ben Sira, in some cases seems to suggest that while suffering and pain is a reality in this world, it was created only for the wicked right from the beginning. But the good things were from the beginning created for both the good and the bad (see Sira 39:25). Nonetheless, Ben Sira seems a bit ambiguous. While in one case he claims that evil and good were created from the beginning, in the other case, he tends to suggest that good is turned into evil for the wicked. He writes, "From the beginning, good things were created for good people, just as evil things for sinners. Basic to all needs of man's life are water and fire and iron and salt and wheat flour and milk and honey, the blood of the grape, and oil and clothing. All these are for good to the godly, *just* as they turn into evil for the sinners" (Sira 39:25–27). A legitimate question could be, did God create both evil and good, or did he only create good that turns into evil for the wicked? Even though Ben Sira does not provide an answer to the mentioned ambiguity, he was ready, according to Daniel Harrington, to postulate that natural disasters brought about by the wind, fire, hail, famine, and pestilence, as well as wild animals and wars, were all instruments of God to punish the wicked.[24]

It is important to highlight, before proceeding, that all wisdom literature did not fully support the retribution theology principle. "The biblical wisdom known as Ecclesiastes or Qoheleth, [...] expressed some skepticism about the truth of the law of retribution. Adopting the persona of King Solomon [the ideal Israelite sage], this author writing in the fourth or third century BC. refuses to accept the assumption that people get what they deserve."[25] Without completely repudiating retribution (Ecclesiastes 7:17), the preacher's life experience has shown him that everything is vanity (Ecclesiastes 1:2). Good or righteous people perish in their righteousness, while wicked people prosper in life (Ecclesiastes 7:15). And at the end of the day, both righteous and wicked die (Ecclesiastes 9:5). At this period of

[23] Ibid, 18.
[24] Cf. Daniel J. Harrington, Why Do We Suffer? 20.
[25] Ibid,18–19.

time, there was not yet faith, belief in eternal life; all the dead (righteous and unrighteous) descended into *Sheol*. "Sheol is the domain of darkness […], pain […], grief […], the absence of the vitality of full existence."[26] For Qoheleth, the retribution law does not always apply. Indeed, vanity of vanities, life is vanity. For the only viable formula we have suggests that the wicked and the righteous are treated the same way at the end of life: they all die, and they all go to Sheol. As for the reward of the good person and punishment of the evildoer, we have no assurance about how that works. Consequently, "Qoheleth goes on to counsel moderation rather than putting too much emphasis on the law of retribution: 'Do not be too righteous, and do not act too wise; why should you destroy yourself?' [Ecclesiastes 7: 16] By being obsessed with righteousness and wisdom, one can miss out on the pleasures of life."[27] In the context of Ben Sira, pain and suffering seem to be a random act.

1.2.2.2 Retribution in the Deuteronomistic Literature

The retribution theology in the traditional five books of Moses is linked and connected to many other theological ideas. To remain faithful to our focus on the place of God in relation to suffering in the scriptures, we will study this section under various topics. In this session, considerable attention shall be given to Deuteronomistic literature (the book of Deuteronomy, the books of Joshua, Judges, Samuel, and Kings) because it plays a pivotal role by serving as the climax of the story of Israel from the call of Abraham, through exodus from Egypt and the wandering in the wilderness to the entry in the promised land.[28] At the core of the Deuteronomistic literature is the ascendancy of Yahweh as the God of Israel and an emphasis on the Law expressed through the covenant. In establishing his covenant with Israel, God also declared his commitment and concern for the nation. The ascendancy of Yahweh, the supremacy and the oneness

---

[26] Casey Deryl Elledge and C. D. Elledge, *Resurrection of the Dead in Early Judaism, 200 BCE–CE 200* (Oxford University Press, 2017), 37.

[27] Daniel J. Harrington, *Why Do We Suffer?* 19.

[28] Cf. Daniel J. Harrington, *Why Do We Suffer?* 21.

of God, interacts in a singularly particular way vis-à-vis the interpretation of joyful and painful experiences of Israel as a nation.

a. God's Concern for Humanity

I cannot emphasize enough that the underlying truth about God's interaction with humanity is the salvation of humankind, the salvation of his suffering people. For the writer(s) of the five books of Moses, this is a truth that cannot be avoided. Moses, in different places, will keep on reminding the people how Yahweh's concern for them had led him (God) to bear them on eagle's wings (Exodus 19:4; Deuteronomy 29:2), to watch over them like an eagle watches over her young (Deuteronomy 32:11). For Moses, God's concern for Israel is primarily lodged in his initiation and fulfillment of the Exodus. Having witnessed the suffering and pain of Israel in Egypt where they had become slaves, God's entrails move within him for Israel, and so he intervenes. He tells Moses,

> I have surely seen the affliction of my people who are in Egypt and have heard their cry because of their taskmasters. I know their sufferings, and I have come down to deliver them out of the hand of the Egyptians and to bring them up out of that land to a good and broad land, a land flowing with milk and honey. (Exodus 3:7–8)

From this time, Yahweh becomes for Israel the God who will be for them what he will be for them. And because he caused to be what he caused to be (God of creation), he was going to prove himself to them as love.[29] It's from this perspective of Yahweh as the concerned God of love who created the universe, endowed it with life and desires the perpetuation of that life in proximity to him, that the law is offered. Daniel Harrington rightly says, "By his many exhortations and law-codes in the book of Deuteronomy, Moses prepared

---

[29] Johann Baptist Metz, "Suffering unto God," 620.

the people for life in the promised land."[30] Consequently, "Near the end of the Book of Deuteronomy, Moses challenges the people to 'choose life.'"[31] He says,

> See, I have set before you today life and good, death and evil. If you obey the commandments of the LORD your God that I command you today, by loving the LORD your God, by walking in his ways, and by keeping his commandments and his statutes and his rules, then you shall live and multiply, and the LORD your God will bless you in the land that you are entering to take possession of it. But if your heart turns away, and you will not hear, but are drawn away to worship other gods and serve them, I declare to you today, that you shall surely perish. You shall not live long in the land that you are going over the Jordan to enter and possess. I call heaven and earth to witness against you today, that I have set before you life and death, blessing and curse. Therefore, choose life, that you and your offspring may live. (Exodus 30:17–19)

Commenting on the passage, Harrington writes,

> In the context of Moses' speech, to choose life means to keep the commandments or the stipulations in Israel's covenant with the Lord God. The rewards for observing these statutes will be God's blessing in the promised land [...] Choosing death means turning away from the Lord God

---

[30] Daniel J. Harrington, Why Do We Suffer? 21.
[31] Ibid.

and serving other gods, and this choice naturally leads to death and adversity.[32]

Yahweh's concern and love for his people leads him to save them from the pain and suffering imposed on them by the Egyptians. However, he does not forget to give them the necessary instructions for a better life in the future.

b. One Supreme and Unique God

A fundamental truth about the covenantal relationship, made of punishments and rewards with Yahweh, is the ascendant supremacy of Yahweh. Initially, Israel was simply the portion of Yahweh, one of the many sons of the El Elyon (the Most High). "For now, Yahweh remains Israel's tribal god, a secondary deity in Elyon's pantheon. Every nation in the ancient Near East had a tribal deity, a god who took care of his people, fought on their behalf in exchange for their unconditional allegiance."[33] "When the Most High gave to the nations their inheritance when he divided mankind, he fixed the borders of the peoples according to the number of the sons of God. But the LORD's portion is his people, Jacob his allotted heritage" (Deuteronomy 32:8–9). But as she (the nation) grew in strength, by developing a monarchy and a military power, her God (Yahweh) received promotion and consequently ascendancy over other gods.[34] It is therefore not strange to see Daniel Harrington stating,

> The early history of Israel in the land of Canaan according to Joshua and Judges is interpreted in the light of its covenant relationship. Israel wins great victories not by its military superiority but by the hand of God. And it fails when it departs

---

[32] Ibid, 21–22.

[33] Thom Stark and John J. Collins, The Human Faces of God: What Scripture Reveals When It Gets God Wrong, 1st edition (Eugene, Or: Wipf & Stock Pub, 2011). 76.

[34] Cf. Thom Stark and John J. Collins, The Human Faces of God, 80–8.

from the Torah. And when one person (Achan) in Joshua 7 defies God's ban on taking the spoil of war, the entire people suffer for his sins: "the people of Israel broke faith in regard to the deposed things ... and the anger of the Lord burned against the people of Israel." (Joshua 7:1)[35]

The Lord of Israel is progressively assuming ascendancy, so much so that he starts to take center stage in the life of Israel. The multiple military wins over the other nations is a sign that the Lord of Israel is powerful, supreme over all the other gods. "Yahweh is said to be so much greater, so much more powerful than other deities, eventually it becomes incoherent even to speak of these other beings as gods at all—so vast is the expanse between their strength and that of Yahweh."[36] And to anger Yahweh (as an individual or as a nation) by not living up to the covenantal law is to attract his severe punishment. By the time of the exile, Israel had so fully articulated the importance of the supremacy of Yahweh that even the most tragic event in its life is attributed to him (God)—not in the sense of Yahweh's defeat, but as his way of punishing for disobedience.

> The belief in Yahweh's supremacy over the other gods had become so firmly established in Israel's theology by the time of the exile that they could not interpret their experiences as Yahweh's defeat without unraveling the very fabric of the national identity. Thus, the exile could not be attributed to the strength of Marduk (the Babylonian god). It was necessary to credit it to Yahweh. It is interpreted as Yahweh's punishment for Israel's sins. Yahweh's supremacy is therefore amplified, and

---

[35] Daniel J. Harrington, Why Do We Suffer? 23.
[36] Thom Stark and John J. Collins, The Human Faces of God, 84.

this is expressed in the solidification of the belief
that Yahweh alone is God.[37]

The supremacy of Yahweh implied his singularity, his oneness.
"Hear O Israel; Your God is one" (Deuteronomy 6:4); all other gods
are but nothing (Deuteronomy 4:35), they are works of human hands
(Psalm 115:4). Yahweh, the God of Israel, becomes an embodiment
of all life's realities. From him comes blessings when he rewards for
good behavior. But from him also comes suffering and pain when he
punishes for bad behavior. "From the perspective of Deuteronomy,
Israel suffers because it failed to worship the Lord God properly, and
failed to keep God's commandments, and Israel prospers only when it
observes God's law [the Torah]."[38] It is no surprise that Schillebeeckx
maintains that Old Testament passages that suggest that God is the
source of good and evil were meant to preserve believers from a dualistic conception of the divine. "In the beginning, God was regarded
as the principle of life and death. The correct intuition here was that
the believer was thus guarding himself against a metaphysical dualism which ascribed the good to God and evil to a 'first principle' of
evil."[39] So we may ask again, where do we place God in the history
of humanity's suffering? We believe the reply is quite simple. For the
Deuteronomistic authors who wholly fought against dualism, against
giving power over Israel to any other divinity, God is at the very
source of pain and suffering. But the leading player, the decider of
God's side concerning suffering, is humanity through its adherence
or failure to adhere to the covenant.

c. Human Responsibility and Evil

The question of the psalmist, "Where is your God" (Psalm 115:
2), was a philosophical question. For beyond asking about the where-
abouts of God in the midst of suffering, the psalmist meant to ask,

---

[37] Thom Stark and John J. Collins, The Human Faces of God, 85.
[38] Daniel J. Harrington, Why Do We Suffer? 22.
[39] Edward Schillebeeckx, Christ, the Experience of Jesus as Lord, (New York:
Seabury Press, 1980), 727.

where did our human actions and attitude place God? The psalmist and Israel knew pretty well that "help comes from the LORD, who made heaven and earth" (Psalm 121:2). To ask where God is when his people face difficulties was not based on some selective dementia from the part of the psalmist, who well knew that help always comes from the Lord. Presumably, the question was founded on the necessity to have a critically introspected self-evaluation. In a sense, one needs to ask, what actions led to the situation of pain and suffering in which I find myself? If we find it, if we can locate it, then we will be ready to understand where God is.

In that outlook, the Mosaic covenant functions as the guiding principle according to which Israel and Israelites could evaluate its conduct and ascertain the place of God whenever they faced difficulties. The law was, therefore, the paradigm for ascertaining what is right and what is not.[40] Knowledge of the difference between what is sinful and what is not implies responsibility. In fact, when Moses reads the Law to them, they reply, "All the words which the Lord has spoken we will do" (Exodus 24:3; Exodus 19:8). By so declaring, Israel accepted to do its part of the covenant that God has established with them. In this regard, Daniel Harrington writes,

> The people are to interpret all 613 commandments in the Torah in the context of God's covenant relationship with Israel. *They represent Israel's side of the covenant.* If Israel observes these commandments as the revelation of God's will, it will be blessed and will prosper. All the statutes are to be viewed in the framework of God's promise at Mount Sinai: "If you obey my voice and keep my covenant, you shall be my treasured possession out of all the peoples" (Exodus 19:5). On the contrary, if Israel sins by idolatry or rebel-

---

[40] Considering the fact that Saint Paul was a student of Gamaliel, it is most likely that he had the right intuition of the understanding of the law. He writes in Galatians 3:19 that the Law was given so that people may know the difference between good and evil.

lion or in some other way, it can expect to suffer
as just punishment of God.[41]

Generally speaking, from the Deuteronomistic perspective, retribution revolved around the principles of God's concern for humanity. In his (God's) concern for humanity, he sealed a covenantal relationship with us declaring himself to be the unique and supreme God who expects some commitment from our side to the covenant. When Israel fails to acknowledge the supremacy and singularity of God and worships other gods, it is punished with pain and suffering. However, a commitment to the one unique God by observing his commandments leads to rewarding blessings.

1.2.2.3. Retribution in Prophetic Literature

I have already mentioned how the exiles—to Assyria (721 BCE) and to Babylonia (587 BCE)—were interpreted as a punishment from God because of the sinful ways of Israel. Because Israel disobeyed God's commandment, Yahweh gave them up to their enemies, the Assyrians and the Babylonians. In the meantime, when Israelites returned from exile, they most likely expected to live a perfect life (see Jeremiah 29:10–14). If they were back to the land that God had given them, it is because they had purged their sins and had been forgiven. In Isaiah 40:2, the prophet writes, "Speak tenderly to Jerusalem, and cry to her that her warfare is ended, that *her iniquity is pardoned,* that *she has received from the LORD's hand double for all her sins.*" It will not be long before Israel realizes that life back in the promised land is not as rosy as they expected it to be. Their experience was that of persistent suffering and obduracy in sinfulness that marked the post-exilic period. Israel remains unable to live up to the expectation of God; they fail in the responsibility to keep their side of the covenant.

However, at various levels, prophets asserted two vital conclusions about the human nature and God's action vis-à-vis the presence

---

[41] Daniel J. Harrington, Why Do We Suffer? 22–23, with added emphasis.

and persistence of suffering in the world. First, they explained that human nature as it is known through its actions will always lead to pain and suffering as retribution. For instance, the exilic prophet Ezekiel will "blame the capture of Jerusalem and the destruction of the temple on the people's sin: 'And because of all your abominations, I [God] will do to you what I have never done'" (Ezekiel 5: 9).[42] For the prophets, it seemed that suffering and pain were here to stay. People will always suffer because they remain wicked. So Jeremiah, a pre-exilic prophet, tells the people of Israel, "Your wickedness will punish you, and your apostasies will convict you" (Jeremiah 2:19).

Second, the prophets also agree that God will destroy suffering. "The prophets refuse to give sin and suffering the last word. Rather, they hold out hope for repentance and a restoration of God's people."[43] Most prophets proclaimed that ignoring their summons to metanoia was tantamount to the threat of God's annihilating judgment.[44] For some, the hope of a sin- and suffering-free world would come only from God, who would destroy the wicked and reward the righteous. Others simply believed that God's obliterating judgment would have to destroy this age and replace it with a new one. In any case, for the prophets, "sin and suffering do not have the last word."[45] God does.

1.2.3. Job's Theology of Suffering

The book of Job is one of the Old Testament books that treats extensively the problem, the mystery of human suffering. It seems that the writer either personally experienced suffering and pain he deemed not to have merited, or he had seen someone innocently suffer. Why do bad things happen to good people, to innocent people? he might have asked. Where is the just and good God when the

---

[42] Ibid, 24.

[43] Ibid.

[44] Cf. Edward Schillebeeckx, The Collected Works of Edward Schillebeeckx Volume 6: Jesus: An Experiment in Christology (London: T&T Clark, 2014), loc. 2664 & 2667.

[45] Daniel J. Harrington, Why Do We Suffer? 25.

innocent is suffering? Harold S. Kushner suggests that to understand the book of Job and the answers provided, one need to take into consideration three propositions. "A. God is all powerful and causes everything that happens in the world. Nothing happens without his willing it. B. God is Just and fair, and stands for people getting what they deserve, so that the good prosper and the wicked are punished. C. Job is a good person."[46] The three propositions point to the dilemma involved in the experience of innocent suffering. Because God is powerful and just, if one suffers, it means s/he has transgressed. This is the line of thought that Job's friends will adopt since they tend to espouse the theology of retribution. They will radically maintain that Job is not as innocent as he pretends to be. Eliphaz asks Job, "Can mortals be righteous before God?" (Job 4:17). In Job 15, Eliphaz accuses Job of arrogance and reiterates his position. "What is man that he can be clean? Or he that is born of a woman, that he can be righteous?" (Job 15:14). For Bildad, the second friend of Job, God's justice is so perfect that it cannot be applied unjustly. In Job 8:3, he asks, "Does God pervert justice? Or does the Almighty pervert the right?" Here, Job is encouraged to understand that his suffering might have been the result of sin. When Zophar, the third friend of Job, enters into the conversation, in Job 11:6 and 11, he explains, "Know that God exacts of you less than your guilt deserves [...] For he knows worthless men; when he sees iniquity, will he not consider it?" Once again, Job faces the torture of accepting that he is not innocent and needs to repent.

The book of Job, however, started by affirming the righteousness of Job. He is described as a blameless and upright man, one who feared God, and turned away from evil (Job 1:1). Even God in the heavenly court boasts of him. He tells Satan, "Have you considered my servant Job, that there is none like him on earth, a blameless and upright man who fears God and turns away from evil?" (Job 1:8). Job is certainly not a sinner as his companions suggest. His misfortunes

---

[46] Harold S. Kushner, When Bad Things Happen to Good People (Knopf Doubleday Publishing Group, 2007), 42–43.

run deeper than the retribution theology that Eliphaz, Bildad, and Zophar are evoking.

It is here important to take some few lines to explain the textual composition of the book of Job. The book is divided into three parts, two of which have the same textual form (prose). First, we have the prose prologue (Job 1:1–2:10). Second is the poetic section, which consists of the discourses of Job and his friends and the two speeches by God.[47] The third part is the prose epilogue found in Job 42:10–17. After a thorough look at the structure as described, one cannot help but agree with scholars who maintain that the author of the book adopted an ancient folktale and inserted in it poems. "Most scholars argue that the author of this [Job's] book took an ancient folktale and reshaped it. The folktale was a familiar story about a legendary wise man who was tested, found to be faithful, and subsequently was rewarded for his faithfulness."[48]

The original folktale adopted by the writer suggests that Job's *suffering is a test*. "Job's perfect life is interrupted by two tests [1:6–22 and 2:1–10] that resulted in his suffering."[49] Satan, with the permission of God, first destroys all the possessions of Job. Job simply answers to his loss by maintaining,: "Naked I came from my mother's womb, and naked shall I return there; the Lord gave, and the Lord has taken away; blessed be the name of the Lord" (Job 1:21). And when Job is tested for the second time with sickness, he still does nothing but patiently accepts his situation. He says,. "Shall we receive the good at the hand of God, and not receive the bad?" (Job 2:10). Job was righteous before the tests came his way, and even after being inflicted, he did not seem to have said anything outrageous against God. In fact, according to Daniel Harrington, "Job interprets his *suffering as a part of human existence*. Though mysterious, his suffering is not unexpected."[50]

What changes the equation is the addition, the inserted poems in the original folktale. Through these poems—except two (the God's

---

[47] Cf. Robin Ryan, God and the Mystery of Human Suffering, 36.
[48] Ibid, 35.
[49] Daniel J. Harrington, Why Do We Suffer? 34.
[50] Ibid, 35, with added emphasis.

speeches)—Job is accused by his friends who also defend God. When these friends defend God and accuse Job of being a sinner, he (Job) cannot take it. He finds their arguments very scandalous. "Whereas Eliphaz seems convinced that Job is the problem, Job in chapter 6, contends that God and his friends constitute the real problem." For him, God is the real cause of his suffering: "For the arrows of the Almighty are in me" (Job 6:4).[51] When Bildad's intervention about God's justice ends, Job has a reply: "How can a mortal be just before God?" (Job 9:2). And Daniel Harrington explains, "Job's formulation here is not so much an appeal to human sinfulness as it is to the unjust situation in which God appears to him to be both judge and adversary. He accuses God of being capricious and elusive [see 9:5–7, 11]. While defending his own innocence ['I am blameless,' (9: 21)], he accuses God of injustice ['he destroys both the blameless and the wicked,' (9:22)]."[52] Job's line of argument remains the same throughout the book; he perceived his pain and suffering as an act of God.

> Job, in chapter 16, responds that God, not Job, is the real problem: "Surely now God has worn me out; he has made desolate all my company" (16:7). From Job's perspective, it is not simply a case of God allowing him to suffer. Rather, God is the agent or the cause of his suffering. Job makes this charge with the help of very violent images: "I was at ease, and he broke me in two; he seized me by the neck and dashed me to pieces; he set me up as his target; his archers surround me. He slashes open my kidney and shows no mercy; he pours out my gall on the ground" (16:12–13).[53]

Despite Job's compelling accusation of God as the source, the cause of his troubles, intriguingly, as the author returns to his origi-

---

[51] Ibid, 37.
[52] Ibid, 38.
[53] Ibid, 39.

nal folktale, he (Job) relies on God for salvation. So in the midst of pain and suffering, of accusation from friends, of his self-defense and blame on God, he prays,

> O that my words were written down! O that they were inscribed in a book! O that with an iron pen and with lead they were engraved on a rock forever! For I know that my Redeemer lives, and that at the last he will stand upon the earth; and after my skin has been thus destroyed, then in my flesh I shall see God, whom I shall see on my side, and my eyes shall behold, and not another. My heart faints within me! (Job 19:23–27)

Commenting on the prayerful passage of Job, Daniel Harrington underscores,

> In ancient Israel a "redeemer" (go'el) acted on behalf of a relative to buy back family property (see Leviticus 25:25), to exact vengeance (see Numbers 35:19–21), or to marry a widow (see Ruth). This is […an] example of Job's desire for a patron or protector. Christians instinctively think of Jesus as this Redeemer and the fulfillment of Job's wish. But in the historical context of the book's composition, the verse most likely refers to God. In his hope against hope, Job wishes that God would take his side and vindicate his innocence.[54]

After a long conversation with God, Job's conception about God's power and justice in the face of suffering is widened and broadened. Even though the widening of Job's horizon does not solve the

---

[54] Ibid, 40.

problem of suffering, Job's health and properties are restored to him (Job 38–42).

1.2.4. Apocalypticism

According to Schillebeeckx, the apocalyptic movement—that is, God destroying history and creating a new one, or God intervening to fundamentally change the history—of the post-exilic period found expression from the realization of the sinful nature of humanity. A sinful nature finds its origin, according to some authors, at the very beginning of humanity, that is, the disobedience of Adam and Eve. Here, the argument is that humankind has always been rebellious; it has always disobeyed God, and it is not about to change. There is no hope for salvation unless God intervenes to alter the course of history fundamentally. Or to replace this history entirely.

> The substance of apocalypticism was characterized by the long experience of human life, an experience which had ceased to look for any improvement in human history. Suffering and every kind of calamity, whether individual or national, were so persistent that one had to postulate at the source of humankind's history a fall of the first man, which snowballed through the ages [...] Thus Satan with his entourage obtained power over this world.[55]

For Daniel Harrington,

> The literature of the Jewish apocalypticism is rooted in the problem of suffering. From a historical perspective, it arose out of the conflict between God's promises to Israel and

---

[55] Edward Schillebeeckx, The Collected Works of Edward Schillebeeckx Volume 6: Jesus: An Experiment in Christology, Loc. 2714.

Israel's political subjugation to a series of foreign empires: Babylonians, Persians, Greeks, Ptolemies, Seleucids, and Romans [...] It is clear [...] as the Book of Daniel shows, that apocalyptic is the literature of dispossessed and oppressed people. According to the apocalyptic perspective, divine intervention could rescue God's people from their present distress and bring about a correspondence between God's promises to the chosen people and the present historical situation.[56]

While in the theology of retribution, there seems to be an active human responsibility that may save humanity from suffering and pain in this world, apocalyptic literature, brackets that responsibility altogether. In the apocalyptic perspective, the power of the evil forces and Satan, even though "under the ultimate control of God,"[57] have reversed, or maybe delayed, the retribution. Now, obedience to the law seems to mean suffering in the here and now, in this world, with the opportunity to enjoy eternity. Daniel Harrington explains, "The apocalyptic solution encourages suffering people to persist in their righteousness, to trust in God and to hope that God will unveil his countenance to the world."[58] Schillebeeckx believed that God's countenance and rewards for the just, as maintained by apocalyptic writers, will be revealed only at the beginning of the eschatological age. He writes,

However, when the eschaton—that is, the radically new age—dawns the boundaries between earthly and celestial history are blurred. Good men now live in company with the angels; they shine like stars in the firmament (Dan. 12:3; Enoch 50:1; 51:4). After the final catastrophe,

---

[56] Daniel J. Harrington, Why Do We Suffer? 71.
[57] Ibid, 72.
[58] Ibid.

> therefore, there is a new state of affairs. Conditions are reversed: those who weep now will laugh; the poor will be rich, the mighty downcast. The paradisal situation is eschatologically restored, and the pious among non-Israelite nations also share in this eschatological age; they share Israel's good fortune, or rather that of the faithful remnant of Israel; for the chosen people is no longer the whole nation, only the devout "holy remnant."[59]

Punishment and reward remain but are deferred to the last judgment or to some other divine intervention.[60] Instead of good and righteous people prospering in this age, they tend to be afflicted with suffering from evil forces that are superhuman.[61] But, "[w]hen God's kingdom comes, then the righteous will be vindicated, and the wicked will be punished or annihilated."[62] Consequently, "[a]ll hope was fixed in the 'turn of the ages,' that is, a sudden divine intervention, which would totally annihilate this history, 'this age' […] so as to create from scratch a brand new heaven and earth, a 'second aeon,' like the earthly paradise before the fall. 'The Most High has created not one aeon, but two'" (4 Ezra 7:50).[63]

From the apocalyptic movement, there are three essential things to keep in mind. First, the existence of pain and suffering in the world is due to sin, which corrupted the order of things, of God's creation. Second, whether human nature is capable or incapable of obedience, life on earth involves pain and suffering. Third, for the apocalyptic movement, pain and suffering are a result of all the sacrifices that one makes, in obedience to the law, for the sake of a better life at the end of time.

---

[59] Edward Schillebeeckx, The Collected Works of Edward Schillebeeckx Volume 6: Jesus: An Experiment in Christology, loc. 2782–2786.

[60] Cf. Daniel J. Harrington, Why Do We Suffer? 72.

[61] Cf. Robin Ryan, God and the Mystery of Human Suffering, 45.

[62] Daniel J. Harrington, Why Do We Suffer? 72.

[63] Edward Schillebeeckx, The Collected Works of Edward Schillebeeckx Volume 6: Jesus: An Experiment in Christology, loc. 2714–2724.

The suffering of the God's people is only temporary, and their vindication is near. How near? The
question "How long?" receives several answers in
[Daniel] 12:5–12, each expressing confidence in
the imminence of the end and each pushing the
precise time further into the future. There are
three timetables: "a time, two times, and half a
time" ([Daniel] 12:7, see 8:14, 9:26–27) = three
and half years; 1,290 days (12:11); and 1,335
days (12:12). The book ends with a promise of
resurrection and vindication for Daniel himself:
"You shall rise for the reward at the end of the
days" (12:12).[64]

The world is already corrupt, and so obedience to God's law
means swimming against the stream, making metanoia, and sacrifices. For instance, when Antiochus IV Epiphanes corrupts Israel by
imposing a pagan cult that prohibits the observance of God's law, the
people are invited to resist (1 Maccabees 2:14–22) even if that means
death (see 1 Maccabees 2:32–38 and 50). In the perspective of the
faithful remnant of Israel, of those who refused Hellenistic assimila-
tion, the pagan cult that amounted to "a desolating sacrilege" or, as
it is traditionally rendered, "the abomination of desolation" was to
be fought.[65] So Mattathias, Judas Maccabaeus the son of Mattathias,
and their followers had to swim upstream, making all the sacrifices
needed to reestablish the worship of Yahweh in a purified temple.

From the perspective of the authors of the books of Daniel and
the Maccabees, suffering and pain are allowed by God for a short
while—perhaps so that the people may be converted, or to give an
opportunity for the people to prove their dedication. But why will a
good God allow his people to suffer?

---

[64] Daniel J. Harrington, Why Do We Suffer? 81.
[65] Cf. Daniel J. Harrington, Why Do We Suffer? 73.

1.2.4.1. Modified Apocalyptic Dualism

Modified apocalyptic dualism is an effort to take up simultaneously the questions of suffering and the omnipotence of God. About this, Daniel Harrington writes,

> While the book of Daniel presents God as allowing the temporal triumph of arrogant foreign rulers, it does not explore the underlining theological implications. One early attempt at putting together the reality of evil and suffering with the omnipotence of God can be described as modified apocalyptic dualism. This approach proposes that while God created the world, it is now under the direction of two subordinate powers (one good and the other evil) until, at the time appointed by God, evil and suffering associated with it will be destroyed forever. This approach is a "dualism" in so far as it posits two opposing powers. It is "modified" because it insists on the ultimate sovereignty of God over all creation. And it is "apocalyptic" since it conveys a revelation about the future course of history.[66]

The very reality that the Deuteronomistic writers never wanted to assert is here asserted. There are lower powers that seem to govern this present age world. Maybe the most precise and most complete presentation of modified dualism is found in the scroll of the Rule of the Qumran Community. There, after insisting on the absolute sovereignty of God, the instructor—most likely, the guide of the Dead Sea community—suggests that God, besides human beings, appointed two spirits, powers to govern the world.[67] Consequently, "[i]n the present, there is a clear division or dualism at all levels. 'All

---

[66] Ibid, 82.
[67] Cf. Daniel J. Harrington, Why Do We Suffer? 82.

the children of righteousness are ruled by the prince of Light and walk in the ways of light, but all the children of falsehood are ruled by the Angel of Darkness and walk in the ways of darkness.' The Angel of darkness is a 'Satan' figure [but more powerful and sinister than in the book of Job], while the Angel of light seems to be Michael or some similar figure."[68]

From the apocalyptic perspective, it seems that the best language for the place of pain and suffering in the world is that of allowance. God allows suffering, either by allowing foreign evil powers to be prosperous or by allowing the prince of darkness, Satan—ruling the world side by side with the angel of light—to have his earthly dominion. But a time will come when God will destroy pain and suffering and reward all who fought to uphold the law of God and all who stood against Satan.

1.2.5. Suffering in the World: John the Baptist's Perspective

Schillebeeckx notes that the personal appearance of John the Baptist, a contemporary of Jesus, "was eschatological in character: the man's whole life is directed to the future, leaving all that precedes it—the past and the present—for what it is, ignoring it and living *wholly by and for the future*. The present is occupied only with metanoia, conversion, exodus, leaving behind all that is and journeying towards that future. What is that future? John does not seem to have proclaimed the kingdom of God."[69]

John's reticence to proclaim the kingdom or the advent of the second aeon is lodged in his understanding that the divine fire of God's coming judgment is going to completely destroy—not purify like in a case of a metal—every chaff and barren tree that does not bear fruit.[70] Schillebeeckx seems to suggest that in John's perspective,

---

[68] Ibid, 83.

[69] Edward Schillebeeckx, The Collected Works of Edward Schillebeeckx Volume 6: Jesus: An Experiment in Christology, loc. 2867–2870–2073.

[70] Cf. Edward Schillebeeckx, The Collected Works of Edward Schillebeeckx Volume 6: Jesus: An Experiment in Christology, loc. 2904.

not even the *Anawim*, the remnant of Israel, bore fruits with the chance of escaping the destructive fire of God's wrath.[71] His baptism just offered a possibility—and not an assurance—of avoiding the approaching catastrophic events of God's judgment. Broadly speaking, "John [was] no purveyor of a gospel or glad tidings of salvation, he [was] a prophet of doom, threatening mankind with looming divine judgment."[72]

God's judgment will be rendered by the coming one, known in apocalyptic circles as the son of man, *Ho erchomenos*.[73] While John remained faithful to the theological orientation of his time, his proclamation of God's painful judgment at the end of time was exponentially magnified (Matthew 3:12). He expected metanoia through his baptism, which would lead to the bearing of fruits. But he strongly felt that the fate of humanity would be utter destruction with wailing and grinding of teeth. "John the prophet forges an intrinsic link between future expectation and ethical-religious commitment—yet from an exclusive perspective of judgment, not from the religious perspective of God's graciousness and love. In that respect, Jesus would not follow John the Baptist."[74]

In John the Baptist's understanding, humanity has a responsibility to bear when we ask where God is. The responsibility of humanity is not even a guarantee of escaping God's judgment either in the present or at the end of time. Strangely enough, John does not even proclaim a world or age where humanity will be free from sin. For John, pain is what we have now. Metanoia and sacrifice is our human responsibility. As for the future, it is uncertain.

---

[71] Cf. Edward Schillebeeckx, The Collected Works of Edward Schillebeeckx Volume 6: Jesus: An Experiment in Christology, loc. 2954.

[72] Edward Schillebeeckx, The Collected Works of Edward Schillebeeckx Volume 6: Jesus: An Experiment in Christology, loc. 2889–2892.

[73] Cf. Edward Schillebeeckx, The Collected Works of Edward Schillebeeckx Volume 6: Jesus: An Experiment in Christology, loc. 2980.

[74] Edward Schillebeeckx, The Collected Works of Edward Schillebeeckx Volume 6: Jesus: An Experiment in Christology, loc. 3058–3061.

1.2.6. Suffering as Sacrifice

Suffering as sacrifice is one motif that cuts across not only the Old and New Testaments when people are trying to make sense of their suffering, but also through the early Christian and modern-day vision of suffering. Daniel Harrington writes, "One common way of imbuing suffering with sense is with the help of the concept of sacrifice."[75] The image of the suffering servant, who sacrifices his life for his people, in the Old Testament is a very inspiring one. According to David Arthur DeSilva, while the theology of one person suffering sacrificially for the sake of others developed during the second temple period, its roots were deeply sunk into the theology of the suffering servant of Isaiah 52 and 53. The belief was that "the suffering and death of the martyred righteous had a redemptive efficacy for all Israel and secured God's grace and pardon for his people."[76] The redemptive efficacy was not just because the martyr dies, but because he voluntarily accepted death through an act of "absolute obedience to the divine will."[77] Consequently, David DeSilva stipulates,

> That the death of an individual could atone for the transgressions of the many remains a possible reading of Isaiah 52:13–53:12, which to a later reader might appear to be spoken not by the Gentile nations to Israel but by a sinful Israelite of a particular righteous person within Israel whose suffering and death are made (by himself Isaiah 53:10b, and by God, Isaiah 53:6b) an offering for the sins of the collective whole.[78]

---

[75] Daniel J. Harrington, Why Do We Suffer? 53.

[76] David Arthur DeSilva, 4 Maccabees (Sheffield, England: Sheffield Academic Press, 1998), 137–138.

[77] John Merlin Powis Smith, "The Biblical Doctrine of Atonement: I. Atonement in Pre-prophetic Israel," The Biblical World 31, no. 1 (1908): 24.

[78] David Arthur DeSilva, 4 Maccabees, 139.

Daniel Harrington explains explicitly that in Isiah 53:4–6:

> That the servant suffered for others is expressed in several ways: "surely, he has borne our infirmities and carried our diseases…he was wounded for our transgressions, caused for our iniquities." That the Servant's suffering had positive consequences for others is also emphasized: "upon him was the punishment that made us whole, and by his bruises, we are healed." It is as if all the punishments due to all the sins of God's people have been visited upon the figure of God's Servant: "the Lord has laid on him the iniquity of us all." And the result of the Servant's suffering is the healing and the wholeness of God's people.[79]

We hear the same arguments of suffering as sacrifice being articulated by the Hasmoneans during the second temple period. The heroic deaths of Eleazar and the seven brothers in 2 Maccabees 7—retold in 4 Maccabees—provide us with such insightful interpretations. The last brother, while about to be martyred, prays, "Like my brothers, I offer up my body and my life for our ancestral laws, imploring God to show mercy soon to our nation, and by afflictions and blows to make you confess that he alone is God" (2 Maccabees 7:37). The concept that one could die in atonement for the sins of the multitude as a theory at this time was lived and expressed. Eleazar made a similar prayer when he too was about to die. "Be merciful to your people and let our punishment suffice for them. Make our blood their purification, and take my life in exchange for theirs" (4 Maccabees 6:28–29).

In the New Testament, there are multiple hints showing us that Jesus is identified as the suffering servant.

> At various points, the Gospels bear witness to the early Christian identification of Jesus as the

---

[79] Daniel J. Harrington, Why Do We Suffer? 59.

servant of God. The elderly Simeon prophesies that the Child Jesus will be "light to the nations" (Luke 2:32; see Isaiah 42:6, 49:6). At his baptism, by John, Jesus is identified by the heavenly voice as "my Son, the beloved; with you I am pleased" (Mark 1:11; see Isaiah 42:1). John the Baptist describes Jesus as "the Lamb of God who takes away the sin of the world" (John 1:29; see Isaiah 53:7, 12). Matthew interprets Jesus' healing activities with the help of Isaiah 53:4: "He took away our infirmities and bore our diseases" (Matthew 8:17). And Matthew quotes Isaiah 42:1–4 in full, in 12:18–21, to shed light on Jesus' ministry and the mixed reception he received.[80]

And because Jesus is identified as the suffering servant, his cross (suffering and death) is interpreted as a sacrifice for the well-being of many. For instance, in Mark 10:45, Jesus is said to have maintained that he came to give his life as a ransom for many. "The blood of Jesus is to be 'poured out *for the forgiveness of sins*' [see 26:28]. On the cross, Matthew's Jesus is mocked for having 'saved others' but being unable to save himself [27: 42]."[81]

Besides the Gospels, Saint Paul also leans heavily on the double theme of the suffering servant and sacrifice as his *modus operandi* in the understanding of Jesus's suffering and death. In his multiple correspondences, Paul explains how: God put Jesus forward as a sacrifice of atonement by his blood (Romans 3:23), and Christ, the one who died for all (2 Corinthians 5:14), died as a sin offering for our sins (1 Corinthians 15:3). In his letter to the Galatians, Paul perceives Jesus as the one who gave himself for our sins to set us free from the present evil age (see Galatians 1:4). In the deutero-Pauline literature, the author also seems to have been cited for asserting that

---

[80] Ibid, 61.

[81] Donald Senior, The Passion of Jesus in the Gospel of Matthew (Wilmington, Delaware: Michael Glazier, 1985), 166.

he suffers for the sake of the Christian community. "I am now rejoicing for your sake, and in my flesh, I am completing what is lacking in Christ's afflictions for the sake of his body, that is, the church" (Colossians 1:24). Commenting on the passage, Daniel Harrington suggests that the letter asserts that "Paul suffered on behalf of the other Christians and rejoiced to do so."[82] While the theme of suffering as sacrifice seems to have been and still is a predominant one in Christians' understanding of pain and suffering, it does not directly address the issues related to the origin or cause of suffering. Instead, the theology of suffering as sacrifice only suggests that people either suffer on behalf of others or that God makes some people suffer for the sake of the well-being of others.

1. 2.7. Suffering in the Gospels

We have already suggested that suffering as a sacrifice is one of the many explanations of suffering that runs through the Old Testament as well as through the New Testament. But since "each of the Gospels revolves around the crucifixion of Jesus,"[83] we would expect that a broader perspective is employed to understand and express the reasons for, and reactions to the arrest, the condemnation, the crucifixion, and the death of Christ. However, because pain and suffering have always been a mysterious reality to comprehend fully, the case of Jesus the Son of God is not different. Consequently, I agree with this observation made by Donald Senior:

> It would be arrogant folly to suggest that what follows will "solve" the riddle of suffering. The passion narratives do not offer packaged answers to the questions created by human agony. But they do offer perspectives and meaning. They show Jesus, the Son of God and child of the uni-

---

[82] Daniel J. Harrington, Why Do We Suffer? 64.

[83] Donald Senior, The Passion of Jesus in the Gospel of Mark (Wilmington, Delaware: Michael Glazier, 1984). (Wilmington, Delaware: Michael Glazier, 1984), 7.

verse, walking the same path of pain and death, yet not broken by it. They portray this representative human, this "new Adam," displaying the many moods of the Christian before death: anguish, lament, peaceful acceptance, stunned silence.[84]

Besides, we are not here pretending to be able to explore all the interpretations that the Gospel writers attribute to the suffering of Jesus.

1.2.7.1. Suffering in Mark

The Gospel of Mark establishes an active link between Jesus's mission and his death. Donald Senior explains, "The death of Jesus is the climax of a life for others."[85] Jesus suffers and dies not because he has chosen to die, but because his ultimate mission of preparing the world for, and establishing the coming of the kingdom of God, was misunderstood and maybe misinterpreted by his contemporaries. Donald Senior clarifies, "So hostile is the opposition to Jesus and his liberating mission that he is accused of being in league with Satan and his exorcisms carried out through the power of evil."[86] In fact, in a conversation with the scribes from Jerusalem, who were Jesus's accusers on the matter (see Mark 3:22), Jesus maintains that his absolute power over the evil spirit is from God and not from Satan. Satan is powerful, but cannot be divided against himself, Jesus explains (see Mark 3:23–26). While Satan might be powerful, Jesus characterizes his power as superior over that of Satan. The proof is that "no one can enter a strong man's house to plunder his property without first tying up the strong man; then indeed the house can be plundered" (Mark 3:27). And since Satan cannot be divided against himself (Mark 3:25), by casting out the evil spirits, Jesus must be

---

[84] Donald Senior, The Passion of Jesus in the Gospel of Mark, 8.
[85] Ibid, 139.
[86] Donald Senior, Why the Cross? (Nashville: Abingdon Press, 2014), 32.

strong enough to bind Satan and plunder his kingdom in order to replace it with the kingdom of God. From the perspective of Jesus's dynamic action against the so-called Beelzebul and his kingdom, one can gather that evil is here the work of Satan, and Jesus, God, is ferociously against it, thus deploying all strategies to fight it and ensure the well-being of humanity.

It is *service for the welfare of humanity that leads Jesus into perpetual combat against evil, pain, and suffering.* He proclaims, "The Son of Man came not to be served but to serve, and give his life as a ransom for many" (Mark 10:45). "Thus this saying of Jesus at a climactic point in the gospel makes the death of Jesus equivalent to 'serving'; the 'ransom' [*lytron*] of his life that Jesus pays is, in fact, his self-transcending giving of life to others."[87] Throughout the Gospel, Jesus is presented as one who serves; he is one who is at the service of the cause of the human race for the kingdom of God. And when he progressively chooses the cross—for "the cross is 'taken up' and not merely endured"[88]—as the climax of his dedicated service to humanity, his Father approves it, and humanity confirms it. It is worth noting that Mark's Gospel does not talk about the annunciation or the incarnation. Jesus's identity is not defined by his divine origin, but by his serving activities that earn his divine "endorsement" and human acknowledgment. The first time Jesus's identity is unveiled is at baptism. We are told a voice came from heaven, "This is my beloved Son in whom I am well pleased" (Mark 1:11). Baptism for Jesus was an act of solidarity with humanity. John gave a baptism of repentance and Jesus, by being baptized, enters into full solidarity with us. This act of sympathy was indeed his first act of service. When Jesus does that, God approves and makes his voice be heard.

At the transfiguration, God once again proclaims Jesus as his beloved Son (Mark 9:7). This declaration of Jesus's identity is important because of what happened in Mark 8:31. It was the first time

---

[87] Ibid, 33.
[88] Donald Senior, The Passion of Jesus in the Gospel of Mark, 140.

Jesus had predicted his passion, death, and resurrection. We read, "Then he began to teach them that the Son of Man must undergo great suffering, and be rejected by the elders, the chief priests, and the scribes, and be killed, and after three days rise again." God speaks again for the second time only when the Son declares how he will ultimately serve (die for the ransom of) humanity.

Finally, when Jesus hangs on the Cross, we witness the ultimate paradox. He (Jesus) who dies because of service, and service for humanity, is acknowledged as Son of God precisely by a Roman centurion whose service was instrumental in crucifying him. The centurion looked up at the dead Jesus who hanged on the cross and said, "Truly this man was God's Son!" (Mark 15:49). Here, for the last time in the Gospel, Jesus's identity is revealed. And it happened when he fulfilled his most significant act of service—his death for our life.

Mark's description of Jesus's life, as well as his portrayal of the passion of Jesus, is encrusted in service. Donald Senior maintains, "All the giving of life that had characterized his [Jesus's] mission until now comes to its climatic point as Jesus gives his own body for the sake of those in need."[89] That is why, "the Passion is safe ground for proclaiming Jesus as Messiah because the Passion, for Mark, expresses Jesus' act of loving service for humanity, the authentic meaning of his Messiahship. Thus, here without distortion, Jesus' redemptive mission is revealed."[90] Here, pain and suffering (the cross) become the result of Jesus's unrelenting serving commitment to the well-being of humanity.

1.2.7.2. Suffering in Matthew's Gospel

Matthew, in his Gospel, besides developing the themes of suffering as a sacrifice and suffering as an unrelenting serving commitment

---

[89] Donald Senior, Why the Cross? 35.
[90] Donald Senior, The Passion of Jesus in the Gospel of Mark, 141.

to humanity's well-being, explored the perspective of *suffering as the result of full obedience to the will of God*. Donald Senior observes,

> One characteristic note in Matthew's portrayal of the ministry of Jesus is his emphasis on the obedience of Jesus to the Father's will - a strong motif of Matthew's Gospel as a whole. The tone is set in the temptation narrative that prefaces Jesus' public ministry. The evangelist portrays Jesus as rejecting the attempts of Satan to turn him aside from his God-given mission. Satan's lure is rejected by Jesus' repeated statements of dedication to God's will (see Matthew 4:1–11). The first words of the Matthean Jesus at his encounter with John the Baptist at the Jordan—"this is necessary to fulfill all righteousness" (3:15)—affirm responsiveness to God's will as the leitmotif of Jesus' entire mission.[91]

As simple as this may sound, it makes our inquiry into the mystery of human suffering very mysterious. Why does one have to suffer if s/he desires to live in complete obedience to the will of God? While Matthew does not provide us with any clear-cut solution on the issue, he does insist that Jesus's passion and death is the result of a Son (the Son of God) who remains faithful to the Father's will, even if that means suffering and pain. So when the passion dawns, "Jesus asserts his commitment unto death [26:1–5]. When the Passover comes, Jesus proclaims the approach of his opportune moment, his *kairos* [26:18], when his obedience would be tested."[92] When at his arrest one of his disciples strikes and cuts the ear of the high priest's servant, Jesus's intervention places before all else the will of the Father found in the fulfillment of the scriptures. He says, "Do you think that I cannot appeal to my Father,

---

[91] Donald Senior, Why the Cross? 43–44.
[92] Donald Senior, The Passion of Jesus in the Gospel of Matthew, 164.

and he will at once send me more than twelve legions of angels? But how then should the scriptures be fulfilled, that it must be so" (Matthew 26:53–54)? In the garden of Gethsemane, Jesus, through his prayers, held again and again onto the will of the Father. "[T]he decisive end of the prayer [in the garden] is Jesus' affirmation of his fidelity to God's will even in the face of death: 'Father…not what I want but what you want' [Matthew 26:39] […] Matthew reinforces this fidelity of Jesus in the words of the second prayer, a prayer not stated in Mark's version: 'My Father, if it's not possible that this cup be taken away unless I drink it, then let your will be what you want' [26:42]."[93] According to Donald Senior, "Matthew's portrayal [of Jesus] is not intended simply to give a compelling example of faithfulness, but is part of a larger canvas which conveys the unique identity of Jesus. Jesus' fidelity marks him as *the* Israelite, remaining true to God where Israel itself may have wavered."[94] At this stage, we can infer the following: If fidelity to God means suffering and pain, then evil is not the work of God. However, evil has made so many give up on God that Jesus through his ministry, condemnation, and death resulting in the resurrection shows that God always has the last word. In a sense, s/he who remains faithful to God still meets, encounters, enjoys God's faithfulness. Suffering may characterize fidelity to God, but God has the last word over suffering.

1.2.7.3. Suffering in the Gospel of Luke

Like Mark and Matthew, Luke's Gospels expands on themes such as sacrifice, service, and fidelity to God as vehicles to explain the cross of Jesus. But it seems the peculiarity of Luke resides in his effort to portray Jesus as a mighty prophet who is coming from God with the power of the spirit and has *the mission to break the power of the evil one.* At the beginning of his public ministry, Luke places Jesus

---

93   Donald Senior, Why the Cross? 46–47.
94   Donald Senior, The Passion of Jesus in the Gospel of Matthew, 165.

in the synagogue of Nazareth. There Jesus is handed the scroll. When he opens it, he reads a passage from the prophet Isaiah in Isaiah 61.

> The Spirit of the Lord is upon me,
> because he has anointed me
> to proclaim good news to the poor.
> He has sent me to proclaim liberty to the captives
> and recovering of sight to the blind,
> to set at liberty those who are oppressed,
> to proclaim the year of the Lord's "favor." (Luke 4:18–19)

Having read the passage, as eyes were fixed on him, Jesus declared, "Today this Scripture has been fulfilled in your hearing" (Luke 4:21). Donald Senior comments, "Several key motifs that will characterize Jesus' mission in Luke are already anticipated in this inaugural scene. First of all, Luke places particular emphasis on Jesus' endowment with the spirit as signaled in his quotation of Isaiah 61 as the keynote of his ministry."[95] While Jesus—the great prophet who has appeared in our midst (Luke 7:16)—lived in conformity with his inaugural proclamation by healing the sick (lepers, paralytics, the woman bent double, etc.), raising the dead (the widow of Nain's son), warning the rich not to forget the poor (the rich man and Lazarus), he was also opposed.

There is one opposing force manifested in two different dimensions. First, "[t]he outcome of Jesus' inaugural proclamation is to trigger the hostility of his hometown audience. Just as the prophets of Israel were rejected and threatened with persecution and death, so the people of Nazareth rise up in indignation and attempt to hurl Jesus off the cliff at the edge of the town [4:29]."[96] The human opposition is not limited to the citizens of Nazareth. There was also Herod Antipas who, according to some Pharisees, was planning to kill him, certainly other religious leaders as well.

---

[95] Donald Senior, Why the Cross? 51.
[96] Ibid, 52.

The second and most important opposing power was the evil power of darkness. "Luke understood the role of Satan as the ultimate source of opposition to Jesus."[97] And Donald Senior continues,

> At one profound level, Luke conceives of the death of Jesus as a final confrontation with the power of evil—a power he had already confronted in the healings and exorcisms of his ministry but was now coming to its final struggle on the cross. The forces arrayed against Jesus are on one level human actors—the religious leaders, Pilate, the soldiers, the crowds and the passerby—but on a deeper level, the driving force that opposes Jesus as God's Holy One and as the spirit-endowed liberator and Messiah is the very personification of evil. As Jesus declares to those who come to arrest him, led by Judas the betrayer, "this is your time, when darkness rules" (22:53).[98]

The opposition to Jesus's liberating plan of the universe runs very deep. It is Satan himself who inspires human actors to fight their liberator. And when human action seems inadequate in achieving what he wants, Satan personally assaults, and Jesus ends up on the cross. Once again, the devil appears to have something to do with suffering and pain in the world, and the cross of Jesus. And Jesus is depicted as one who fights the powers of darkness that inflict pain and suffering on humanity.

1.2.7.4. Suffering in the Gospel of John

John portrays Jesus's death as an act of love for the world (see John 3:16–17). But one may not be far off the mark by maintaining that in John's Gospel, the cross of Jesus is an act of loving sacrifice

---

[97] Ibid, 53.

[98] Ibid, 53–54.

for the sake of life, the life of the world. Here the emphasis is not sacrifice but love for the life of the world.

On the one hand, we may note that in the twenty-one chapters of the Gospel, the word "Life" appears forty-three times. This is a clear indication of how important Life is in Jesus's actions and interactions with human beings. Expressions such as, "I am the bread of life" (John 6: 35), "I am the living water" (John 4; John 7), "I am the Good Shepherd who lays down his life for his sheep" (John 10: 11), "I am the resurrection and the Life" (John 11: 25), "I am the way the truth and the Life" (John 14: 6) magnify the purpose of Jesus's life-giving activities.

On the other hand, it is impossible to read the Gospel of John without realizing the importance that love plays in God's life-giving redemptive interaction with humanity. One of the most known passages in the Gospel ("For God so loved the world, that he gave his only Son, that whoever believes in him should not perish but have eternal life" [John 3:16]) is but a small glimpse into this truth. Consequently, Donald Senior writes,

> The God-given and cosmic mission of Jesus, the Word made flesh, is to reveal God's *redemptive love* for the world. That love is expressed in both the words and deeds of Jesus. Because the heart of Jesus' message is God's redeeming love, the most eloquent and unimpeachable expression of that love is Jesus' death on the cross, which is, in fact, the ultimate realization of love—the laying down of one's life for the sake of another. Because the death of Jesus is the ultimate expression of God's love for the world, it becomes the completion of Jesus' mission and the source of his exaltation and triumphant return to his Father.[99]

---

[99] Ibid, 62–63, with added emphasis.

The "deep logic"[100] of John's Gospel is, therefore, life out of love for the sake of the world. Jesus is cited by John to have said, "Truly, truly I say to you, if a grain of wheat does not fall to the ground and die, it remains only one; but if it dies, it bears much fruit" (John 12:24). The agricultural parable that Jesus uses here is foundational in understanding the logic of dying to keep and give life. The parable contains a remarkable soteriological value: the grain is Jesus, who, like the grain of wheat, has to die in order to become fountain and source of abundant life. Life comes from death, and from death love is manifested. By dying, the grain preserves and perpetuates life. Caiaphas prophetically expresses the same logic when addressing the issue related to Jesus's accusation by the Sanhedrin. "Caiaphas, who was the high priest that year, said to them, 'You know nothing at all. Nor do you understand that it is better for you that one man should die for the people, not that the whole nation should perish'" (John 11:49–50).

The fact that John establishes the logic of a loving offer of one's life for the sake of the life of the multitude does not mean he (the author of the Gospel) thinks that Jesus committed some sort of suicide. Instead, like other Gospel writers, John identifies some forces that were directly or indirectly responsible for the cross of Jesus:

> John's Gospel recognizes other driving forces in the body of the gospel narrative that lead to the crucifixion of Jesus. Opposition to Jesus breaks out at the very beginning of the gospel narrative at the cleansing of the temple (2:18–20), intensifies after John 4 and comes to the boiling point in the aftermath of the raising of Lazarus when the chief priest decides to arrest Jesus and have him put to death (11:53). The intent to "kill" Jesus on the part of the religious leaders occurs several times in John's account and gives the opposition

---

[100] Ibid, 62.

to Jesus a particularly bitter edge (see 5:14; 7:1, 19, 25; 8:22, 37, 40).[101]

Apart from the religious leaders, Romans (Pilate and the Roman troops) are also described by John at different levels as ferocious opponents that led to his condemnation (John 19: 16) or/and to his execution. "Roman troops carry out Jesus' crucifixion and, at the request of the religious leaders and agreed to by Pilate, ensure that Jesus and those crucified with him are dead before the onset of the Sabbath [19:31–37]."[102]

One of Jesus's own disciples, the one who was to betray him, is also identified by John as an opponent of Jesus. However, in this case, Judas is considered an instrument of the devil.[103] For, even though Jesus did choose all of his apostles, one, the one to betray him, is a devil (John 6:70–71). And John himself will state that it is the devil who provoked Judas, the son of Simon, to betray Jesus (see John 13:2). When at the Last Supper Judas received a piece of bread from the hand of Jesus, John affirms, "Satan entered into him [Judas]" (John 13:26–27). Judas, being the devil or one manipulated by the devil, works tirelessly to betray Jesus. This is an action in which he eventually succeeds.

More importantly, John points directly to the active work of Satan directly leading to the death of Jesus. Donald Senior explains, "In contrast to the Synoptic Gospels, John's account does not portray Jesus as an exorcist. Rather, Satan lurks behind the scenes, fomenting hatred, encouraging deception and lying, and driving humans to oppose and ultimately attempting to destroy Jesus, God's message."[104] And he concludes, "Although John's Gospel will not refer again in his narrative to the explicit role of Satan as the cause of Jesus' death, it is clear that through the agency of both the religious leaders who virulently oppose Jesus and through the betrayal of Judas, one

---

[101] Ibid, 67–68.
[102] Ibid, 68.
[103] Cf. Donald Senior, Why the Cross? 68.
[104] Ibid, 68.

of the Twelve, Satan will assault Jesus with deadly force."[105] From John's perspective, the logic of life out of love for the sake of others is reinforced by the activities of the devil to destroy Jesus. However, according to the Gospel, Jesus still has control over the entire situation. He proclaims, "No one takes it [his life] from me [Jesus], but I lay it down of my own accord. I have authority to lay it down, and I have authority to take it up again" (John 10:18).

1.2.8. St. Paul's Theology of Suffering

At the very center of the entire Pauline theology is the crucified Lord. In many instances, Paul affirms and reaffirms his commitment to the centrality of the crucified Lord in his theological perspectives. For instance, in 1 Corinthians 2:2, he stipulates, "I decided to know nothing among you except Jesus Christ and him crucified." Further in 1 Corinthians 1:23, he writes,"[W]e preach Christ crucified, a stumbling block to Jews and folly to Gentiles." We may also look at passages like Galatians 6:14. It is, therefore, not surprising when Donald Senior explains, "Paul speaks frequently of the death of Jesus or the suffering of Jesus and in virtually every instance he has in mind Jesus' death on the *cross*."[106]

Paul's commitment to the crucified Lord is rooted in his faith that the death of Christ reveals something fundamental about the nature of God in his interaction with humanity. Before proceeding, it is fundamental to explain that "[w]hile the resurrection of the Crucified Lord is essential for the saving power of the cross, Paul puts more emphatic focus on the *cross* of Jesus as the eloquent and startling revelation of God's very nature and the extraordinary way God effects human salvation."[107] Said differently, Paul does not separate the cross from the resurrection; he always tends to keep those two events together while focusing or delving deeper into the suffering of

---

[105] Ibid, 69.
[106] Ibid, 79.
[107] Ibid, 80.

Jesus, the cross. For Paul, through the cross, God confounds human wisdom and reveals power in weakness.[108]

> In giving them the message of salvation, the God of Jesus Crucified was being faithful to God's paradoxical logic: "But God chose what the world considers foolish to shame the wise. God chose what the world considers weak to shame the strong. And God chose what the world considers low-class and low-life—what we considered to be nothing—to reduce what is considered to be something to nothing. So, no human being can brag in God's presence" (1 Cor 1:21–29). In using such terms as "foolish," "weak," "low," and "considered to be nothing," Paul is surely thinking not only of the social standing of the Christians but of the Crucified Jesus himself.[109]

In a sense, Paul reveals that the power of God, the glory of God, is revealed through human weakness.

While God can and does reveal his glory and/or wisdom of salvation through human weakness and suffering, God is not responsible for the weakness of humanity. It is through the first Adam that sin entered into the world, and through that sin, weakness, suffering and death made their way into human life. According to Donald Senior, sin in Paul's theology does not always refer to individual immoral acts. He explains, "A key to Paul's thought is his understanding of 'sin.' By 'sin' Paul does not refer primarily to individual immoral acts but to a quasi-cosmic force that entered the world with Adam's sin and through the accumulative power of evil, reigns over the world, holding humanity in its grip and condemning human beings to death."[110] In Paul's understanding, sin and its consequences

---

[108] Cf. Donald Senior, Why the Cross? 83.
[109] Ibid, 84.
[110] Ibid, 89.

(weakness and death) are taken up by God and transformed into an instrument of our salvation. And this God achieves through one man, just as sin and its consequences came through one man (see Romans 5:17). Greeks say, "Fire does not extinguish fire." But for Paul—who thinks that God's foolishness is wiser than human wisdom (see 1 Corinthians 1:25)—there is a reverse situation: another *Fire* much more powerful is what is needed to break the power of *fire* and thus save humanity. "Paul is convinced that through his death on the cross—an act of consummate love—and through his resurrection from the dead, Jesus Christ radically breaks this deadly power of sin and paves the way for those who believe in Jesus to be able to experience freedom from death and to enjoy abundant new life with God."[111]

Since God used—without creating—the human weakness of Jesus to save humanity from the power of sin, and since we are members of the body of Christ (see 1 Corinthians 12), the possibility that we suffer for the sake of the salvation of humanity is a high possibility. Our incorporation into the body of Christ through baptism cannot leave us without implications. Just like him (Paul), we need—if we want to rise with Christ—to bear in our bodies the marks of Christ and accept the suffering that comes with discipleship.

The theology of God using weakness to break the power of Satan and revert the consequences of sin is not the only perspective on suffering in Paul's writings. Paul, in other instances, understands the cross as bringing about a divine exchange between God and man, which has a behavioral implication for humanity. "On God's part, there is through the representative action of Christ, forgiveness of our sins; on our part, there is justification as a result, yet as a way of life as well."[112] Expressions such as Christ was made sin so that we may be justified (2 Corinthians 5:21), Christ became curse for us (Galatians 3:13), and died for us (2 Corinthians 5:14–15), are but a little glimpse into the complexity of Paul's conception of the cross.

---

[111] Ibid, 89.

[112] Jan Lambrecht, Second Corinthians (Collegeville, Minn.: Liturgical Press, 1999), 101.

1.2.9. Highlight of Other Themes on Suffering in the New Testament

1.2.9.1. Suffering as Discipline from God in the Hebrews

The theme of *suffering as a discipline* from God is not a novelty of the author of the letter to the Hebrews. The first instance where we have this perspective of suffering as discipline is in the book of Proverbs. The wisdom writer says, "My son, do not despise the Lord's discipline or be weary of his reproof, for the Lord reproves him whom he loves, as a father the son in whom he delights" (Proverbs 3:11–12). The author of the Letter to the Hebrews alluding to the Proverbs has a similar perception of suffering. He states,

> "My son, do not regard lightly the discipline of the Lord, nor be weary when reproved by him. For the Lord disciplines the one he loves, and chastises every son whom he receives." It is for discipline that you have to endure. God is treating you as sons. For what son is there whom his father does not discipline? If you are left without discipline, in which all have participated, then you are illegitimate children and not sons. Besides this, we have had earthly fathers who disciplined us and we respected them. Shall we not much more be subject to the Father of spirits and live? For they disciplined us for a short time as it seemed best to them, but he disciplines us for our good, that we may share his holiness. For the moment, all discipline seems painful rather than pleasant, but later it yields the peaceful fruit of righteousness to those who have been trained by it. (Hebrews 12:5–11)

The Christian community is here exhorted to understand that their suffering is a discipline from God, who like a caring parent disciplines it for its own good in order that they may share in his holiness.[113] Robin Ryan in expanding the subject of suffering as a discipline from God explains, "The interpretation of suffering as divine discipline is, of course, an ambiguous one. It is simply one interpretation among many others. If all suffering were understood in this way one could ascribe to God the worst forms of evil that human beings inflict upon one another."[114] Did the author of the Hebrews intend to blame God for the suffering of the community? Maybe the author of the Hebrews was simply suggesting that the suffering endured by the community, even though inflicted by others, was intended or permitted by God who wants to discipline his people.

1.2.9.2. Suffering as a Purifying Force in First Peter

Suffering as a purifying force from God is not a new theme that the writer of First Peter created. Already in Isaiah 48:10, we read, "Behold, I have refined you, but not as silver; I have tried you in the furnace of affliction." The author of First Peter, taking a cue from Isaiah and Wisdom, portrays suffering as purifying force, the prominent theme of his exhortation to the suffering communities of northern Asia Minor.[115] He tells his audience, "For a little while you have had to suffer various trials, so that the genuineness of your faith—being more precious than gold that, though perishable, is tested by fire—may be found to result in praise and glory and honor when Jesus Christ is revealed" (Peter 1:6–7). Commenting on the passage, Robin Ryan writes, "The notion of suffering as trial was part of the Wisdom tradition of the Hebrew scriptures [for example, Wisdom 3:5–6]. The purifying effect of suffering is one of the reason that Christians can maintain a spirit of joy throughout their endurance of hardship. Their faith is becoming more authentic—more radiant—

---

[113] Cf. Robin Ryan, God and the Mystery of Human Suffering, 68.
[114] Ibid, 68–69.
[115] Cf. Robin Ryan, God and the Mystery of Human Suffering, 70.

by means of this experience."[116] Here, the suggestion is that through suffering one gets the opportunity to model his/her life according to Jesus. "The believer must witness to his or her faith by doing good, knowing that such conduct may lead to unjust suffering, as it did for Jesus. Indeed, Jesus is presented as a true exemplar of faith in adversity: 'When he was abused, he did not return abuse; when he suffered, he did not threaten; but he entrusted himself to the one who judges justly' [1 Peter 2:23]."[117] Suffering becomes a means through which one has the opportunity to identify with Christ. An identification that helps him/her to get purified by patiently sharing in the suffering of Christ. It seems to me that the writer of First Peter does not accuse God for the presence of suffering in the world. All he does is to suggest that purification can be achieved through suffering, leading to modeling oneself on Christ. Or if one is already molded to Christ, then purification is achieved through sharing in the passion of Christ.

Where is God? This is one of the fundamental questions that people ask when they face pain and suffering. God, in one way or another, finds himself or, if we prefer, finds his name in the midst of people's effort to make sense of what they are experiencing as pain and suffering. In that perspective, the Bible has multiple responses. The lament tradition is simply concerned about actively coping with suffering by complaint to God and trusting that he who is powerful will always come to the rescue of humanity. The theology of retribution teaches, in some cases, that God punished humankind for its disobedience, in other instances that humankind simply faced the consequences of its wrong choices. Prophets placed the entire burden of the presence of pain and suffering in the world on humanity. Because we are wicked and are resisting metanoia, we will always suffer. However, at the end of the day, God will come to the rescue of humanity. For the apocalyptic literature, this world is so corrupt that to live according to the commandments may mean suffering and pain. But for those who, despite the adversities of this world,

---

[116] Ibid, 70.
[117] Ibid.

remain faithful to God, eternal happiness, a homeland without pain and suffering awaits them. Modified apocalyptic dualism might have been the very first instance where a different force, apart from God, is attributed the power of making humanity suffer. Satan and his maleficent angels are given some kind of independent existence from God, but under the ultimate control of God who will crush them at the end of time. The New Testament has a panoply of responses to address the mystery of suffering, that of the Son of God in particular. Suffering takes the connotations of, inter alia, sacrifice, service, obedience, destruction of the power of evil, offer of life, justification, transformation, discipline, purification, and all for the sake of all.

Chapter 2

Classical Theism: The Two Evils and Their Origin

A s seen in the previous chapter, the Bible explains in various ways the origin of evil and the attitude portrayed by humanity when faced with suffering and pain. Inspired by some of the biblical perspectives on suffering, renowned theologians like St. Augustine and St. Thomas Aquinas endeavored to defend God from any responsibility in human suffering. The classical philosophical and theological teachings about the goodness, the love, and the immutability of God made it almost impossible to blame him (God) for any evil or suffering in the world. However, the belief in God's justice made it possible, in some cases, to think of suffering as a punishment from God. In an attempt to explain pain and suffering in the world without taking away the power of God, St. Augustine, and later on St. Thomas Aquinas, maintained the principle of two evils (natural or evil suffered, and moral or evil done). But before that, they postulated that evil is nothing but the privation of good.

2.1. Evil as the Privation of Good

Without intending to probe the entire classical theology on the immutability, impassibility, and omnipotence of God, I will focus on some proposals by classical theologians like St. Augustine and St. Thomas Aquinas. Both influenced and continue to influence theological discourse on the mystery of suffering. Taking a cue from Plato and Plotinus, Neoplatonism asserted that evil is not a substance in itself but a privation. Christian thinkers, St. Augustine and St.

Thomas Aquinas included, adopted this philosophical principle as a way of defending the uncompromising goodness and unity of God the creator.[118] The belief that evil is the privation of good became the basis for repudiating its substantive existence, and consequently its creation. In a sense, theologians wanted their audience to understand that evil is not an essence. Robin Ryan makes this same point by citing Basil of Caesarea, who wrote a treatise entitled *God Is not the Author of Evils*. In that treatise, Basil of Caesarea, according to Ryan, explained that people should not imagine that evil has a substance particular to it.[119] "Wickedness," he continued, "does not exist like some living thing. We cannot set it before our eyes as something existing. Evil is a privation of the good."[120]

St. Augustine expressed the same principle of evil as being the corruption of a substantially good thing and not a substance in itself. Ryan explains that St. Augustine perceived evil as a sickness or a wound, thus representing the absence of the good that should be present.[121] Similarly, Thomas Aquinas in his writings "rejects the notion of an absolute principle of evil in the universe." He insists that "the sovereign good is the cause of the whole being. Being as such is the gift of the Creator. There is no contrasting principle that is the source of evil."[122] By asserting the non-substantial existence of evil, these theologians simultaneously maintained the unity of God. Unlike the Gnostics, who established a difference between God the Creator, the source of evil, and the God the Redeemer of the New Testament, the principle of good, classical theism was able to maintain that there is one God who is the God of creation and redemption. Even though evil is not a substance, it remains a reality. How do we account for its presence in the world? Augustine and Aquinas suggest the theory of the two evils.

---

[118] Cf. Robin Ryan, God and the Mystery of Human Suffering: A Theological Conversation across the Ages (NY: Paulist Press, 2011), 84.

[119] Cf. Robin Ryan, God and the Mystery of Human Suffering, 85.

[120] Ibid, 85.

[121] Ibid, 86.

[122] Ibid, 127.

2.2. *God, Humanity, and the Two Evils in St. Augustine*

St. Augustine is known as one of the most important defenders of the Church. He is prominently known to have defended the Church against the heretical teachings of his time. "Since the history of its foundation, Christianity has been endowed with two constitutional embarrassments which over and over again have tempted Christian theology into dualistic concepts."[123] If in the Old Testament, after Israel became monotheist, an effort was made to fight dualism and attribute everything to God, it became more and more difficult to do the same in the early Church. According to Johann Baptist Metz, the difficulty of the early church to successfully maintain the oneness of God in all things was based on the heretical teachings of Marcion, who "drove a wedge between the Old Testament tradition of the creator God and the New Testament language of redemption."[124] Making use of the gnostic dualism between the creator God, who is a lesser god (demiurge), and the redeemer God of the New Testament, Marcion argued that the delay of the Parousia is due to "the timelessness [*Zeitlosigkeit*] of salvation but also the irredeemability [*Heillosigkeit*] of time."[125] In a nutshell, the universe is made of binaries: the demiurge responsible for the imperfect world of pain and suffering in time and the redeeming God accountable for the timeless salvation.

While it is true that St. Augustine lived and taught in a Church that was built up in opposition to Marcion,[126] he was also challenged in his lifetime by the heretical teachings of Manichaeism. Ryan explains,

> Augustine grappled with the problem of evil throughout his life. His temporary association with the Manicheans as an auditor in the sect reflects his search for an answer to the dilemma

---

[123] Johann Baptist Metz, "Suffering unto God," 616.

[124] Ibid.

[125] Ibid, 616.

[126] Cf. Johann Baptist Metz, "Suffering unto God," 616.

of evil. Manichaeism provided a straightforward solution to this dilemma, positing two principles, a source of goodness and a source of evil.[127]

In an anti-Manichean tract entitled *On Free Choice of the Will*, he set out to answer the questions of his friend Evodius. The latter begins the conversation by asking *whether God is the source of evil*.[128] A plain yes to this question would imply the cruelty of God and limit him to being merely the creator. Augustine walks a fine line as he tries to reply to his friend. He distinguishes two evils.

> We speak of evil, Augustine observes, in two senses—as evil that one does as a voluntary act and as evil that one suffers. If one believes "that God is good," he claims, "God does not do evil." "Also," he continues, "if we admit that God is just (and it is a sacrilege to deny this), He assigns rewards to the righteous and punishments to the wicked—punishments that are indeed evil for those who suffer them. Therefore, if no one suffers penalty unjustly [this too we must believe since we believe that divine Providence governs the universe], God is the cause of the second kind of evil, but not the first."[129]

By this distinction, Augustine seemed to suggest that through what humanity does—of course, sinfully—evil is carried out.

Humanity is blamed for the first evil. Commenting on the human encounter with the first evil, as suggested by the distinction of St. Augustine, John Thiel writes, "Our conscience calls us to task for breaking the moral law, causing harm to ourselves, to others, or

---

[127] Robin Ryan, God and the Mystery of Human Suffering, 85.

[128] Cf. John E. Thiel, God, Evil, and Innocent Suffering: A Theological Reflection (NY: Crossroad, 2002), 4.

[129] Ibid.

both."[130] Richard Miller, I believe, has an excellent explanation of Augustine's understanding of the origin of the first evil. He explains that for St. Augustine, the sinful attitude of the human will to cling to mutable realities as if they were immutable is one of the reasons for the first evil in the world.

> According to Augustine, evil arises when we seek to overcome our fundamental lack as mortal creatures by attaching ourselves to changeable goods in excess of their quality and being. We confuse mutable for immutable goods, drawn as we are to objects of beauty that are finite and contingent in our restless quest for enduring happiness. In the process, we elevate the value of temporal goods to a status they neither deserve nor can sustain. Augustine understands that such desires are sinful because they are disordered. They fail to draw the correct measure in our world and leave us unhappy and unsatisfied. Indeed, such pursuits of happiness are doomed to fail given that we have tethered our hopes to goods that are fated to decay. Our desires will remain unquenched, and our sense of internal order will remain off-kilter insofar as we fail to draw delight and direction from God as the Supreme Good. Confused about the qualitative difference between eternity and time, between unchanging and changing goods, we attach our loves to gifts of death. In these terms, Augustine concludes the first book of *Confessions*, after recounting his years of infancy and early youth: "In this lay my sin, that not in [God] was I seeking pleasures, distinctions, and

---

[130] Ibid.

truth, but in myself and creatures, and so I fell headlong into pains, confusion, and errors."[131]

Thus, Augustine uses his own life experience to explain the origin of evil in the world. If we all focused—by living a morally upright life according to the commandments—on God the supreme good, we could all avoid the suffering and pains that come from attachment to ephemeral earthly goods or desires. Augustine then goes ahead in the second book of the *Confessions* to tell a story about stealing pears with his friend. Through that story, Augustine suggests that sometimes we bring suffering and pain to others just by an arbitrary desire to witness to their losses. For at the end of the story, "he confessed, 'I was greedy for another's loss without any desire on my part to gain anything or to settle a score?'"[132] And Richard Miller concludes, "For Augustine, the ground of arbitrary, unmotivated evil in the will is surd, dark and inaccessible, mute and irrational."[133] While evil here is still understood as originating from humanity, Augustine seems to suggest that, apart from the fact that one has the freedom to behave that way, the reasons for such evils are absurd. For some strange reason, we cannot explain why, in some cases, some want to see others suffer. It is also plausible that through the recounting of the experience of stealing pears, Augustine was simply trying to explain suffering as a privation of the good that should be done.

In book three of his *Confessions*, he explains the second evil, the one that one undergoes or suffers rather than perpetrates, as the work of God for a just reason.

> In the opening passage of *On Free Choice of the Will*, Augustine goes so far as to say that God is the cause of [the] second kind of evil. The sufferer does not cause disease, or ill fortune beyond human agency, or the frailty of old age, or the

---

[131] Richard B. Miller, "Evil, Friendship, and Iconic Realism in Augustine's 'Confessions,'" The Harvard Theological Review 104, no. 4 (2011), 387–388.

[132] Ibid, 389.

[133] Ibid.

death that comes from natural causes sooner or later in life. Only God wields power capable of inflicting such suffering. And yet, though God is the cause, such suffering is not innocent.[134]

An attentive reader may realize that Augustine seems to be caught up in a dilemma. He acknowledges the power of the one unique God of the Christians to inflict pain and suffering, yet he desires to defend and maintain God's goodness. Subsequently, Augustine proposes that the suffering God inflicts is not caused by him but by humanity, since it "is the just recompense for the perpetration of the evil of which all are guilty."[135] It is not, therefore, surprising to read Johann Baptist Metz maintain that Augustine "locates the *cause as well as the responsibility for evil and suffering in the world exclusively in humanity* and the history of guilt that is rooted in its no to God. Hence God, God's self especially the creator God is left out of the theodicy question."[136] Vis-à-vis the goodness of God that we all postulate, the problem of the persistence of pain and suffering is the resultant evil from humanity's no to God.

In Augustine's mind, there is nothing like innocent humanity and innocent suffering. The so-called innocents are not that innocent. For all have sinned (Romans 5:12). With this appeal to Paul's letter to the Romans, Augustine established his doctrine of Original Sin. "As a Child of Adam and Eve, the doctrine holds, no human person is innocent, for all share in their sin through birth and so are inescapably guilty."[137] Before the sin of Adam and Eve, which wounded humanity as a whole, we lived a perfect life, without pain and suffering. According to Ryan,

Augustine had an exalted understanding of the state of the first human beings in paradise. They

---

[134] John E. Thiel, God, Evil, and Innocent Suffering: A Theological Reflection, 6–7.

[135] Ibid, 7.

[136] Johann Baptist Metz, "Suffering unto God,"616, with added emphasis.

[137] John E. Thiel, God, Evil, and Innocent Suffering: A Theological Reflection, 12.

were immune from physical ills and had extraordinary intellectual gifts; they lived in the enjoyment of God, with surpassing natural powers and the gifts of the grace necessary for obeying God. They not only had free will (*liberum arbitrium*) but also true freedom (*libertas*), which for Augustine means free will oriented towards goodness.[138]

The reality of life changed when Adam sinned.

In Augustine's mind, [the first] sin was a grievous fault, a heinous crime that adversely affected the entire human race and all of human history. Augustine thought that the ancient ecclesial practice of baptizing infants and including exorcisms in the baptismal rite was a proof that all people are born infected with sin. He was convinced that because of original sin human nature has been wounded.[139]

In a nutshell, for Augustine, the sin of Adam and Eve was, kind of, a mutation that modified the entire genetic coding of humanity. Freedom and free will have been assailed and are now disordered. The only way forward, the only way to salvation is God's grace given by Christ the Good Samaritan. "All people are in desperate need of Christ the Good Samaritan, who alone can heal our nature, orient us to the good and empower us to live as disciples of Jesus."[140]

Augustine also believed that through the Original Sin, a penalty was imposed by God on humanity as a whole. Our God is a just God. Consequently, God's justice demanded that sinful humanity be penalized.

---

[138] Robin Ryan, God and the Mystery of Human Suffering, 112.
[139] Ibid.
[140] Ibid.

In the *City of God*, for example, he reflects on the travails of this life, which begin in the infancy and last until death. Even baptized babies, the most innocent of God's creatures in Augustine's mind "suffer many ills, and in some instances are even exposed to the assaults of the evil spirits." Babies are born with terrible disabilities that cannot be understood as a penalty for personal sin. The process of learning for children is an ordeal that usually necessitates severe discipline. For Augustine, the harsh condition of this world can be understood only as the consequence of the disorder in creation that resulted from the misuse of human freedom at the origin of human history and the ensuing penalty that was imposed on sinful humanity as a whole. "From Augustine's standpoint, God's justice is under attack by anyone who thinks that human misery, from infancy on, is *not* the consequence of sin."[141]

Augustine's argument about the origin and cause of suffering puts all the blame on humanity. First, the sin of Adam affected humanity. Then, the penalty of the sin of Adam affects humankind in general. And third, our use of freedom is disordered. Augustine's denial of innocent suffering, according to John E. Thiel, "allows the character of God to stand amidst the most disturbing, and utterly common suffering encountered in history. Simply put, the denial of

---

[141] Ibid, 113. See also St. Augustine, The City of God, trans. Marcus Dodds (NY: Random House, 1950), 21, 14. In citing Elizabeth Clark, Robin Ryan demonstrates how she believed that Augustine's doctrine of original sin was primarily founded on his own experience of evil and suffering in the world (see Robin Ryan, God and the Mystery of Human Suffering, 111). See also Elizabeth Clark, The Origenist Controversy: The Cultural Construction of an Early Christian Debate (Princeton, NJ: Princeton University Press, 1992), 227–244.

innocent suffering lets the Christian God be the Christian God."[142] Johann Baptist Metz explains the same reality by maintaining that

> the Augustinian conception is no doubt only intelligible as a counter to Manichaeism and Gnosticism. *Not God but humanity become sinful bears sole responsibility for a creation that has been distorted by suffering, shot through with suffering.* Augustine's strong doctrine of freedom arises from an apologetic intent: an apology for the creator God.[143]

It appears to me that for the apologetic Augustine, while God is capable of evil, he is incapable of inflicting unjust suffering and pain. If there is such an abundance of suffering in the world, it is because in God's justice we deserve it.

For Augustine, though God is all-powerful and all-good, he must have a say in the living condition of humanity. Since Augustine was concerned about repudiating the bifurcation between God the Creator and God the Redeemer proposed by Gnosticism and Manichaeism, he has to look for an alternative. For the God of the Christian faith, whose very being is goodness, mercy, and love, simply cannot be reconciled with the agent of suffering.[144] Accordingly, St. Augustine inserts the famous word of *permissibility* in his treatment of the mystery of suffering. God does not do evil; he simply permits evil. But God permits evil only for the sake of something good. On the issue regarding God's permissibility of suffering in Augustine, Ryan observes,

> Augustine makes an important affirmation of the faith that will be quoted by later Christian theologians, including Thomas Aquinas: "For

---

[142] John E. Thiel, God, Evil, and Innocent Suffering: A Theological Reflection, 12.
[143] Johann Baptist Metz, "Suffering unto God," 616, with added emphasis.
[144] Cf. John E. Thiel, God, Evil, and Innocent Suffering: A Theological Reflection, 11.

the Almighty God, who, as even the heathen acknowledge, has supreme power over all things, being himself supremely good, *would never permit* the existence of anything evil among his works, if he were not so omnipotent and good that he can bring good even out of evil."[145]

In a sense, Augustine moves the cause of pain and suffering from God and places the entire responsibility—with the exception of God's permission—on the innate (original sin), deliberate, as well as arbitrary transgressions of humanity and the consequences that go with it. While God is not the cause of human suffering, he does permit it, for the sake of justice. But because of his love for humanity, and through his ultimate power, he will always bring something good out of suffering.

About the death of Jesus, Augustine held that "the Father and the Son, and the Spirit of both, work all things equally and harmoniously; yet *we are justified in the blood of Christ, and we are reconciled to God by the death of His Son.*"[146] For him, the sin sacrifice made by the Son was for the sake of the reconciliation between humanity and God. "Augustine defines sacrifice as 'every work which is done that we may be united with God in holy fellowship, and which has a reference to that supreme good and end in which alone we can be truly blessed.' [...] He interprets the death of Jesus, the mediator between God and humanity as the perfection and fulfillment of all the sacrifices."[147] While Jesus makes a sacrifice so that we may be united or reconciled with God, Augustine realizes that such unity may not be achievable unless divine justice is satisfied. So he writes,

By the justice of God in some sense, the human race was delivered into the power of the devil; the

---

[145] Robin Ryan, God and the Mystery of Human Suffering, 86. See Augustine's handbook The Enchiridion on Faith, Hope, and Love. The emphasis is mine.

[146] St. Augustine, On the Trinity, XIII: 15, ed. Philip Schaff, (n.d. 1887), 295, with added emphasis.

[147] Robin Ryan, Jesus and Salvation: Soundings in the Christian Tradition and Contemporary Theology (Collegeville, Minnesota: Liturgical Press, 2015), 64.

sin of the first man passing over originally into all of both sexes in their birth through conjugal union, and the debt of our first parents binding their whole posterity [...] But the way in which man was thus delivered into the power of the devil, ought not to be so understood as if God did this, or commanded it to be done; but that He only permitted it, yet that justly. For when He abandoned the sinner, the author of the sin immediately entered. Yet God did not certainly so abandon His own creature as not to show Himself to him as God creating and quickening, and among penal evils bestowing also many good things upon the evil. For He has not in anger shut up His tender mercies. Nor did He dismiss man from the law of His own power, when He permitted him to be in the power of the devil; since even the devil himself is not separated from the power of the Omnipotent, as neither from His goodness. [148]

In this sophisticated statement, Augustine desired to demonstrate that by divine justice we were allowed to be under the grip of the devil, but that justice is satisfied through the sacrifice of the innocent Son of God. Ryan explains,

For Augustine, the devil acquired rights over humanity when Adam and Eve sinned, and God permitted them (and all humanity contained in them) to be delivered into the devil's power. [...] In response to this catastrophe, God chose to free the human race by an act, not of divine power, but of divine justice [...] Because the devil killed an innocent man, he lost his power over human-

---

[148] St. Augustine, On the Trinity, XII:16, ed. Philip Schaff, (n.d. 1887), 295–296.

ity. Augustine argues that it was only right for the devil "to free these people through the one who was guilty of no sin, but whom he undeservedly afflicted with the punishment of death."[149]

Thus, the death of Jesus becomes the ransom for the salvation of humanity. Jesus pays the price of divine justice through the unjust attack of the devil.

Finally, Augustine also wishes to convey that the death of Jesus was equally meant to be a trap for Satan. Besides the fact that Jesus's death satisfied divine justice, it also served as a means to enmesh the devil.

> The devil jumped for joy when Christ died, and by the very death of Christ the devil was overcome: he took, as it were, the bait in the mousetrap. He rejoiced at the death, thinking himself death's commander. But that which caused his joy dangled the bait before him. The Lord's cross was the devil's mousetrap: the bait which caught him was the death of the Lord.[150]

According to Augustine, the death of Jesus, which is the sacrifice that fulfills all sacrifices, served as a ransom to satisfy divine justice and ensnare the devil.

Augustine might have realized that even though he was living three centuries after the death of Jesus, evil and suffering were still an active reality in the world. Unable to give any other explanation for the actual presence of suffering in the world, he leaned on the principle of *totus Christus* (the whole Christ). The theorem maintains that because we are part of the body of Christ, whatever he suffered, we

---

[149] Robin Ryan, Jesus and Salvation, 66. See Augustine, On the Trinity, XIII: 12.16.

[150] "Christ's Descension into Hades to Destroy Death," http://classicalchristianity. com/2011/04/23/christs-descension-into-hades-to-destroy-death/ accessed on April 6, 2018.

too suffer in us, and whatever we suffer, he too suffers in us.[151] When commenting on the closeness of Christ to the suffering members of his body as expressed by St. Augustine, Ryan writes,

> Augustine's conviction about the profound union between Christ and the church led to his exquisite reflections on the intimacy between the risen Christ and all suffering members of his body. This belief appears to be more foundational and perhaps far more significant than Augustine's interpretations of suffering as testing, punishment for original sin, and so forth. The fact that God caused the Word to be the head of the body means that for Augustine God is in the closest possible solidarity with the suffering members of his body.[152]

In conclusion, for Augustine, humanity is indeed responsible for the presence of pain and suffering in the world. God could only be blamed—if it were not for divine justice—for allowing or permitting suffering. But even in permitting suffering, God is not a sadist; he always brings out something right out of it. And finally, God is ever present, always close when we suffer.

2.3. God, Humanity, and the Two Evils in Thomas Aquinas

Thomas Aquinas leaned heavily on the theology of St. Augustine. Like Augustine, he maintained that there is no absolute principle of evil as such in the world.

> Aquinas rejects the notion of an absolute principle of evil in the universe. He insists that

---

[151] Cf. Robin Ryan, God and the Mystery of Human Suffering, 114–115.
[152] Ibid, 115. See also St. Augustine, Exposition of Psalm 62, 2.

> "the sovereign good is the cause of the whole
> of being." Being as such is the good gift of the
> Creator. There is no contrasting principle that is
> the source of evil [...] like Augustine, he main-
> tains that evil] is, rather the privation of being;
> it is the absence of something that ought to be
> present for the integrity of a thing.[153]

Ryan explains that for Aquinas, the order of God's creation is absolute goodness. "The first and last word about the universe is goodness, since everything that exists has its source in the creator who is supreme goodness. [Aquinas] asserts that 'evil belongs neither to the integrity of the universe nor serves its development, except incidentally because of an accompanying good'" (*ST* I, 48,1, ad 5).[154] Besides maintaining the goodness of creation, and the absence of a principle of evil, Aquinas makes a distinction between two kinds of evil: *malum poenae* (pain) and *malum culpae* (fault) or evil suffered and evil done.[155]

The evil suffered (natural or physical), while still a privation of good, is viewed by Thomas Aquinas as indirectly willed by God for the sake of the overall good of creation.[156]

Ryan writes,

> God creates "a world in which natural evil is
> always a matter of there being nothing but good
> derived from God." Aquinas speaks of God caus-
> ing evil suffered in the lives of human beings for
> the sake either of correction or justice. Thus, he
> talks of God as a surgeon who amputates a limb
> in order to save a person's body. Just so the divine
> wisdom inflicts pain to prevent fault.[157]

---

[153] Ibid, 127. See Thomas Aquinas, Summa Theologiae I, 48, 1, and 49, 3.
[154] Ibid, 127.
[155] Cf. Robin Ryan, God and the Mystery of Human Suffering, 127.
[156] Cf. Robin Ryan, God and the Mystery of Human Suffering, 128.
[157] Ibid. See Davies, The Thought of Thomas Aquinas, 96.

It does not take a special gift to realize that for Aquinas, the evil suffered is both caused and permitted by God. But God does not create or randomly allow that evil. Instead, he (God) always has the ultimate good in mind. The finality of every suffering and pain caused by God is always the common good of humanity.

As far as the evil done is concerned, Aquinas, like Augustine, traces its origin to humanity. "[E]vil done arises completely from the human side. Its origin is not to be traced to God in any sense. 'Hence the evil which lies in the defective activities or which is caused by a defective agent does not flow from God as its cause.'"[158] But before getting to this conclusion, Aquinas factors into the discussion the doctrine of human freedom. "Since human freedom is not simply autonomous but theonomous, that is, made possible by God, posited by and received from God, then it cannot ultimately be responsible for the history of suffering in the world."[159] For Johann Baptist Metz, human freedom being a gift from God works in and through him (God) who makes it possible or allows it. If God makes human freedom possible, if God permits human freedom to operate, he may be termed, in cases of its wrongful use, the enabler of human suffering. In the perspective of the origin of human freedom, Robin Ryan, commenting on Aquinas, suggests, "God can be termed the cause of moral evil only to the extent that God creates people, preserves them in being, and empowers them to act."[160] To avoid God being completely drawn into the picture of moral suffering, because for him God could not be directly involved in evil, Aquinas will interject the famous scholastic distinction of God simply permitting such evil without being directly the cause of it.[161] God permits moral evil because he has created us with a free will, freedom to choose that he does not desire to interfere with. "Having bestowed individual freedom, 'God permits men and women to commit their own personal sins.' Grace may try to dissuade from evil, but human will prevails.

---

[158] Ibid, 129. See Summa Theologiae I, 49, 2.
[159] Johann Baptist Metz, "Suffering unto God," 617.
[160] Robin Ryan, God and the Mystery of Human Suffering, 129.
[161] Cf. Robin Ryan, God and the Mystery of Human Suffering, 129.

God has chosen not to interfere with this freedom."[162] Johann Baptist Metz finds Thomas Aquinas's argument of God's refusal to interfere with human freedom, especially with sinful human freedom, as apologetic. He writes, "The much-used differentiation in scholastic theology between permitting and causing sinful freedom sounds in this context more like a feeble apologetic distinction."[163]

Aquinas understood original sin as the privation of original justice. For him, original justice entailed four essential elements: (1) perfection of human nature, human freedom included. Ryan explains, "This state of original justice was for Aquinas a gift divinely bestowed upon human nature in the parents of the human race. It was not something owed to Adam and Eve by reason of nature. It did, however, entail the perfection of human nature, including freedom from suffering and death, the integration of human desires [appetites], the gift of charity in the will."[164] (2) The gift of the perpetual presence of God's grace. For Aquinas, the gift of God's grace made possible the harmony between the different powers of the human person and God. He explains that through the gift of God's grace bestowed on humanity at the beginning of time; the body was submissive to the soul, which was submissive to the reason, which in turn was submissive to God.[165] "In this graced condition, the first human possessed all the virtues. Their being was completely oriented to God and to obedience to the divine will."[166]

(3) Aquinas believed that original justice also entailed immunity from suffering. "Original justice also entailed immunity from suffering. Adam 'was immune from it [suffering] both in body and in soul, just as he was immortal, for he could have kept suffering away as much as death if he had persisted without sin'" (*ST*, I, 97, 2).[167] (4) Finally, while Aquinas maintained that original justice was a state

---

[162] Ibid.

[163] Johann Baptist Metz, "Suffering unto God," 617.

[164] Robin Ryan, God and the Mystery of Human Suffering, 131.

[165] Cf. Robin Ryan, God and the Mystery of Human Suffering, 130–131. See Thomas Aquinas, Summa Theologiae I, 95, 1.

[166] Ibid, 131.

[167] Ibid, 13. Note that "ST" stands for Thomas Aquinas's Summa Theologiae.

of natural happiness, he also insisted that the natural happiness did not include a beatific vision but a loftier knowledge of God than that possessed by human beings after the fall.

According to Aquinas, with the sin of Adam and Eve (original sin), all these four conditions for original justice became disordered and wounded.

> Original sin is "a disordered disposition growing from the dissolution of that harmony in which original justice consisted." (*ST* I–II, 82, 1). He [Aquinas] likens this disordered disposition to a bodily illness. Human nature has become sick because of the effects of the sin that occurred at the very origins of human history. In this condition, the powers of the soul have become disturbed. Drawing on the classic image of "wounds," Aquinas speaks of the wounds of ignorance, malice, weakness, and concupiscence. Ignorance damages human reason, malice wounds the will, weakness affects the irascible appetite (the capacity to face situations that are difficult), and concupiscence wounds the concupiscible appetite (the attraction to things that are desirable). Death and other forms of human suffering are also the results of original sin (*ST* I–II, 85, 5).[168]

Thomas Aquinas has sometimes been ambiguous about the effect of original sin on humanity. While in some cases he agrees that original sin leads to suffering, pain, and death, in others—at least in one instance in the *Summa Theologiae*—he tends to take an alternative position. For instance, Robin Ryan notes, "In addressing the question whether death and other bodily ills are the effects of sin, he

---

[168] Ibid, 132.

cites an opposing position that claims that if this were the case then baptism and penance, by which sin is removed through sacramental grace, should also remove death and bodily ills. People living in the state of grace should no longer experience suffering and death."[169] For Aquinas, grace and its five effects—of (1) the healing of the soul, (2) the willingness to do good, (3) the efficacious performance of the good willed, (4) the perseverance in the good, (5) the attainment of glory[170]—are what is needed for a transformative understanding of the plight of humanity. The grace given to humanity through the sacraments, based on the death and resurrection of Jesus, works not in a magical way, but through the wisdom of God. "Thus it must be that subjection to suffering remain for a time in our bodies that in conformity with Christ we may merit the freedom from suffering proper to the state of glory."[171] Just as the Son of God suffered died and rose, and through his death and resurrection God's grace is given to us, so are we invited to configure our lives to the crucified and risen Lord. "For Aquinas, the Christian is meant to configure his or her life to the crucified and risen Lord and, through union with Christ be delivered from suffering in eternal life."[172] Aquinas does suggest to Christians to identify with the suffering Lord if they expect to one day live suffering and pain-free life.

When it comes to understanding the passion of Jesus, Aquinas has multiple interpretations. He interprets the passion as a sacrifice for the redemption of sinful humanity. But he also embraced the theory of satisfaction. Robin Ryan explains, "Aquinas draws upon the theory of satisfaction worked out by Anselm of Canterbury in the latter's *Cur Deus Homo*. He thinks that one of the ways to express the meaning of the saving work of Christ is to speak of Christ as making satisfaction for the debt owed to God by the human race because of sin."[173] While Aquinas believed that God could have enacted his

---

[169] Ibid, 133.
[170] Cf. Robin Ryan, God and the Mystery of Human Suffering, 133.
[171] Thomas Aquinas, Summa Theologiae, I–II, 85, 5, and 2, in Robin Ryan, God and the Mystery of Human Suffering, 134.
[172] Robin Ryan, God and the Mystery of Human Suffering, 134.
[173] Ibid, 136.

salvation in many different ways, since he is only answerable to self, he (Aquinas) considers the cross the best way for the salvation of humanity from sin. "[T]he passion of Jesus was the most excellent way to liberate humankind from sin because it showed us how much God loves us, provided an example of humility and obedience, and restored human dignity."[174] For Aquinas, the most important thing in the passion of Christ, the salvific element of the passion, is not his pain and suffering as such, but the obedience and charity that Christ demonstrated by accepting the cross. For this reason, "he consistently highlights the *obedience* and *charity* of Christ as the true source of salvation."[175] In the Christology of Aquinas, "there is no glorification of human suffering [...] Mary Ann Fatula highlights this salient theme in Aquinas, commenting, 'Thomas saw that Jesus' death saves us not because it was full of pain, but because it was full of love.'"[176]

Here again, the Christian God, who is a good, loving, just, and all-powerful God, is allowed to be. While Aquinas takes little steps further by suggesting God in some cases as the cause of suffering and pain, he is also quick to suggest that it is for the overall good of God's creation. In other instances, Aquinas emphasizes the freedom of humanity, both before and after original sin, that God does not interfere with, even though he gives his grace. Consequently, when humanity's actions lead to pain and suffering, God merely permits or allows it, without necessarily being the cause of it.

St. Augustine and St. Thomas Aquinas developed a foundational theology about the mystery of human suffering. The progress that they made in distinguishing the two types of evils and their origins is very instructive, even though it does not solve the problem of evil. Faced, just like generations before them and generations after, with the fact of the abundance of suffering and pain in the world, they were able to formulate two underlying indices for understanding

---

[174] Ibid, 137.

[175] Ibid.

[176] Ibid. This idea of Mary Ann Fatula can be found in her book Thomas Aquinas: Preacher and Friend (Collegeville, MN: Liturgy Press, 1993), 68.

of suffering. First, God permits, allows, or causes evil, not in a kind of random manner, but for the sake of an ultimate good. Second, by configuration or identification with the suffering and risen Christ, we are assured of a future without pain and suffering.

Chapter 3

The Humanization of Christ in the Middle Age Spiritualities

O ne of the biggest and perhaps the most critical debates of the early Church was that of the nature of Jesus. In the background of the conversation about the nature of Jesus was that of his ability or inability to suffer. If Jesus was human like us, then we can easily hold that he did indeed suffer. If he was divine like others maintained, then the affirmation of the immutability of God does not allow one to postulate that Jesus suffered. While the councils of Nicea (325), Ephesus (431), and Chalcedon (541) clearly declared Jesus to be true God and true man, theological investigations were mostly interested in convincing people about the divinity of Jesus. The humanity aspect seemed to have been taken for granted since Jesus was a historical figure, even though the true humanity of Jesus was discussed at Constantinople I and Chalcedon. As time went on, the Christologies became more and more sophisticated and detached from the reality of the day-to-day living of Christians. It took the practices and spiritualities of a non-sophisticated medieval Christian population to rediscover and reconnect with the human Jesus.

In the previous chapter, I established to a great extent, in the theologies of Thomas Aquinas and St. Augustine, how Jesus was viewed and talked about. Jesus, the Son of God, came and died as a sin-offering. He died to trap the devil or satisfy the Father for the sins of humanity. The academic statements about the life, death, and resurrection of Christ took similar formulation. In fact, in "A Meditative Spectacle: Christ's Bodily Passion in the *Satirica Ystoria*," Roest Bert gives a summary of the seven theological formulations clarifying the reasons for the death of Jesus from St. Augustine to the Middle Ages. These are the following:

> First of all, the death on the Cross was the proper medicine to deal with illness which harassed mankind: what Adam had lost through a tree, Christ regained. Second, Christ has chosen the Cross to show his love, a maternal kind of love which extends to friends and foes alike, disregarding all self-concern. Therewith, Christ made reconciliation possible through his own blood. Third, the Cross was chosen to arouse love in the heart of men, for Christ's suffering demanded compassion. Fourth, the death on the Cross was an example of perfect virtue, which not only took no heed of death itself but also spurned all fear for its most gruesome sort. Fifth, Christ had chosen the Cross to prepare a snare for the devil. The Cross should, therefore, be seen as a fishing rod or a limed twig—with the bleeding body of Christ as a bait. Sixth, the Crucifixion was necessary to extend the healing power of Christ's passion to the four parts of the world, even as far as the very ends of paradise and hell, so that their doors might be opened. Seventh, the Cross was chosen as the symbol of Christ's power, and as the figures of his victory, just as the emperor carries his scepter. And Christ had ascended the Cross like a teacher who climbs into the *cathedra* or like a preacher who climbs the pulpit. Thus he had carried out and shed tears from a high position so that he could be heard by all, and all should be moved without excuse.[177]

---

[177] Bert Roest, "A Meditative Spectacle: Christ's Bodily Passion in the Satirica Ystoria," in The Broken Body: Passion Devotion in Late-Medieval Culture, ed.

The truth, however, was that all these systematic stipulations seemed utterly aloof to the reality of the medieval Christian. "Taken together, [the seven reasons] presented the medieval reader with a fair amount of theological knowledge about the Passion. But presumably, they were not sufficient to provoke in the reader the right attitude."[178] It would not be an exaggeration to claim here that "the popular culture [...] was something very different from the rationalistic debate centered at Paris or Oxford. And yet there exists such a thing as 'climate of opinion,' and 'paradigm shifts' do occur."[179] In his book, *Ten Ways the Church Has Changed: What History Can Teach Us about Uncertain Times*, Christopher Bellitto suggests that in the Middle Ages "a fundamental shift [...] occurred in the way people identified with Jesus, Mary, the saints, the Eucharist, and their Christian brothers and sisters at home. Spirituality changed dramatically because people began to see Jesus not as their final judge, but as a suffering, historical human being."[180]

3.1. Tracing the Paradigm Shift

The paradigm shift was mediated by a certain number of factors, ranging from theology, spirituality, to the day-to-day living of the lay faithful. At the academic level, the turn of the millennium that announced the beginning of the Middle Ages witnessed the final disappearance of the followers of Arius. Arius had developed a theology that suggested that Jesus was not divine like the Father. For him, Jesus the Son of God was begotten (*gennètos*)—an expression he used in the generic sense of 'produced' (*gènetos*), but understood in the

---

R. M. Schlusemann, Bernhard. Ridderbos, and A. A. MacDonald, Mediaevalia Groningana; 21 (Groningen: Egbert Forsten, 1998), 37–38.

[178] Ibid, 38.

[179] Ross Dealy, The Stoic Origins of Erasmus' Philosophy of Christ, 1st edition (Toronto; Buffalo; London: University of Toronto Press, Scholarly Publishing Division, 2017), 248.

[180] Christopher M. Bellitto, Ten Ways the Church Has Changed: What History Can Teach Us about Uncertain Times (Boston, MA: Pauline Books & Media, 2006), 168.

specific sense of "made," "created"[181]—by the Father at a specified period of time. Jesus in lay language would have been termed as the highest and first creature of all the creatures that God ever created. Arius's Christology was rejected, and Jesus, at the council of Nicea, was proclaimed *Homoousios*, that is, to be of the same nature with the Father. After the council, Arianism did not die but persisted at the margins of the Church denying the divinity of Christ. At the beginning of the Middle Ages, with their "final disappearance [...] laypeople and theologians grew more comfortable with the gentle Jesus of the Gospels, as they had been at the very beginning of Christianity a millennium before."[182] From now on, people no longer needed to be reactionary or defensive of Christ's divinity against Arians who denied it. Theologians, as well as laypeople, who paid much attention to the divinity of Christ could as well pay a lot of attention to the humanity of Christ without the fear of being labeled Arians or heretics.

At the social level, the Middle Ages was marked with a lot of pain and suffering. The population of Europe was swiftly growing, but the economic situation was not improving at the speed of the population. Unemployment was very high, and different incurable diseases were plaguing Europe. Worth mentioning here is "the rapidly evolving and dire social situations, brought about most especially by the Black Death, which carried off a third of the population of Europe."[183] There were also frequent wars that led to the death of thousands of people. Faced with such situations of pain and suffering, the question no longer seemed to be who is responsible for all the evil in the world. Rather, people were looking for a faithful companion in misery. They were searching for a God who was closely tied to their own difficult lives as, most especially, the peasants struggled simply to live from day to day.[184] It is no surprise Gerald O'Collins

---

[181] Cf. Jacques Dupuis, Who Do You Say I Am? Introduction to Christology (Maryknoll, NY: Orbis, 1994), 84.

[182] Christopher M. Bellitto, Ten Ways the Church Has Changed: What History Can Teach Us about Uncertain Times, 168.

[183] Ross Dealy, The Stoic Origins of Erasmus' Philosophy of Christ, 252.

[184] Cf. Christopher M. Bellitto, Ten Ways the Church Has Changed: What History Can Teach Us about Uncertain Times, 169.

maintains that the defense of the genuine humanity of Jesus was a task that the ordinary medieval Christian assigned to himself/herself. "[I]t was left to popular devotions to defend [Christ's] genuinely human existence and experience. Thus the devotion to the Christmas crib, the stations of the cross and the devotions to the sacred heart witnessed to the ordinary faithful's instinctive attachment to the authentic humanity of Jesus."[185] A humanity that mirrored, to a great extent, their own plights.

3.2. The Influence of St. Francis of Assisi

Jesus became the man of sorrow, the Man-God who new pain and suffering, just as it is being experienced now. At this stage, "[a]rt, songs, sermons, and Passion plays depicted Jesus as the man of sorrow, humility, suffering, and service. The Christians could more easily identify with these aspects of Jesus than those of the glorified Son of God."[186] There seemed to have been an act of going back to the Gospel stories. It was time to bring them—and not theories and doctrines—to the limelight; it was time to, once again, give life to these stories. "This focus on the Gospel made devotion 'evangelical' and 'practical.'"[187] Sensuality, practicality, and devotions led people to publicly display their emotional attachment to the humanity of Christ by spiritual devotional plays and by their styles of life. Saint Francis of Assisi was an excellent example of that reality. His devotion to the humanity of Christ led him to propose to John of Greccio the staging of the nativity scene for the celebration of Christmas. History holds that Francis told John of Greccio—a Christian, of course:

> If you want us to celebrate the present feast of our
> Lord, at Greccio, go with haste diligently prepare
> what I tell you. For I wish to do something that

---

[185] Gerald O'Collins, "What Are They Saying about Jesus Now?," The Furrow, 1981, 203–211, 204.

[186] Christopher M. Bellitto, Ten Ways the Church Has Changed: What History Can Teach Us about Uncertain Times, 168.

[187] Ibid, 169.

will recall to memory the little Child who was born in Bethlehem and set before our *bodily eyes* in some way *the inconvenience of his infant needs*, how he lay in a manger, how, with an ox and ass standing by, he lay upon the hay where he had been placed.[188]

For the humble and poor Francis, who was particularly close to the people, incarnation as a truth taught by the official Church doctrine was not enough to either evoke pious devotion or display the difficulties of the birth situation of Jesus. For the sake of devotion, imitation, and the poor masses, the event that took place more than 1,200 years before needed to be represented before "*our bodily eyes.*"

It was in the presence of such a lively display of the birth of Jesus that St. Francis proclaimed and preached the word of God, during Christmas. Expressions used were simplified and dramatized to facilitate understanding and imitation.

[St. Francis] preached to the people standing about, and he spoke charming words concerning the nativity of the poor King and the little town of Bethlehem. Frequently too, when he wished to call Christ *Jesus,* he would call him simply the *Child of Bethlehem,* aglow with overflowing love for him; and speaking of the word *Bethlehem,* his voice was more like the bleating of a sheep [...] Besides when he spoke the name *Child of Bethlehem* or *Jesus, his* tongue licked his lips, as it were, relishing and savoring with pleased palate the sweetness of the words. The gifts of the Almighty were multiplied there, and a wonderful vision was seen by a certain virtuous man. For

---

[188] John Raymond Shinners, ed., Medieval Popular Religion, 1000–1500: A Reader, Readings in Medieval Civilizations and Cultures 2 (Peterborough, Ont., Canada; Orchard Park, NY: Broadview Press, 1997), 73–74, with added emphasis.

> he saw a little child lying in the manger lifeless, and he saw the holy man of God [St. Francis] go up to it and rouse the child as from a deep sleep. This vision was not unfitting, for the Child Jesus had been forgotten in the heart of many; but by the working of his grace, he was brought to life again through his servant St. Francis and stamped upon their servant memories.[189]

Through the nativity scene, St. Francis desired to once again bring to life in the memory of the people the reality of the sublime mystery, but also demonstrate the humility of God who in love and charity came to be at the service of humanity by becoming one like us. Consequently, Christ (the Anointed One) becomes simply the *Child of Bethlehem*. Bethlehem becomes *Bethle hèèèèèèèèm*.[190] With all this before our eyes, no one will miss the grandeur of such great a mystery. But there is also the *love, humility, and the suffering* that accompanies God's decision to become one of us, to be at our service.

Once the nativity was materialized in the eyes of the populations, nothing could stop the pious dramatization of all the other stages of the life, death, and resurrection of Jesus. With St. Francis's nativity scene, his explication of the nativity and the visions of medieval Christians, it became obvious that what was important for people was not Christology, but the physical life of the Jesus who lived and walked the streets of Galilee and Jerusalem.

3.3. Passion's Plastic and Verbal Art

I propose here that the stigmata that St. Francis received in 1224 was a significant event that catapulted people's desire to imitate Jesus. I shall return to this aspect when I discuss the stigmata in the fourth chapter. Here it will suffice to stipulate that "[i]ndividuals longed for union with the suffering Christ. St. Francis' stigmata [...]

---

[189] Ibid, 74.
[190] The bleating of sheep.

was held to be the visual sign of an instant where this union had been accomplished."[191] The spiritual experience of the transcendent as experienced by St. Francis was mediated by pain and suffering. Francis achieved his union with Christ through the experience of receiving the painful marks of the Cross. Thus, his experience put at the center stage and almost verging on obsession, the physical suffering of Christ.[192] Bert Roest explains,

> For St. Francis, as well as late-mediaeval religious enthusiasts, "God seemed to attach more weight to love manifested in suffering than love displayed in other ways. Suffering was the means par excellence for demonstrating this love: this was the rule for Christ, and consequently for his saints as well." In consequence of this, these prospective saints attempted a continuous re-enactment of his suffering—one so thorough that eventually the ultimate visible signs of Christ's perfection became visible and tangible on their bodies. After Francis's practical re-enactment of the life of Christ on earth, the bleeding human body was henceforth central: it was what Christ and man had in common and was the actual battlefield on which the salvation of the soul was contested. The mortification and castigation of the flesh therewith became the occasion for salvation.[193]

"In general, late medieval homilies and guidance literature construct a world in which the reader or listener is brought to a new understanding of her or his relationship to God and neighbor

---

[191] Ross Dealy, The Stoic Origins of Erasmus' Philosophy of Christ, 249.

[192] Ibid, 249.

[193] Bert Roest, "A Meditative Spectacle: Christ's Bodily Passion in the Satirica Ystoria," 31.

encountering the living flesh of the wounded Jesus."[194] Suffering or preferably bloody literature was the order of the day. In that perspective, Ross Dealy distinctively observed,

> While in the early Middle Ages thought regarding Christ's passion did not dwell on his suffering and there was little interest in his humanity, a major shift, represented by an immense and widely circulated body of literature, occurred in the period 1100–1500. Over time these "devotionalist" accounts of Christ's death, emphasizing his physical suffering and pain, became ever more elaborate. The theme also pervaded tools for meditations, such as prayer books, paintings and other forms of art, poetry, plays in various setting, liturgy, and music. While Giotto's paintings, around 1300, brought to bear on the passion a greater naturalism, and realism than found previously, painters of the later fourteenth and fifteenth centuries tended to develop this realism by depicting in grotesque details the intensity of the pain.[195]

The only piece of the life of Jesus that seemed appealing to the medieval Christian was the stations of the Cross. Even artworks and writing that depict the entire life of Jesus gave exaggerated attention to his passion. For instance,

> Latin texts of the Passion treatises were among the first and most frequently printed. Books that cover the entire life of Christ also focused on the Passion, particularly important being *Meditationes vitae Christi*, a late thirteenth-century Franciscan

---

[194] Ellen M. Ross, The Grief of God : Images of the Suffering Jesus in Late Medieval England (NY: Oxford University Press, 1997), 30.

[195] Ross Dealy, The Stoic Origins of Erasmus' Philosophy of Christ, 246–247.

work emanating from northern Italy, and *Vita Christi* of Ludolphus of Saxony (d.1377), written between 1348 and 1377. Eleven of one hundred chapters of the *Meditationes* are taken up with the Passion [...] Bestul explains why: "the late medieval fascination with the physical particularities of the suffering of Christ is everywhere apparent, perhaps nowhere more prominently than in the section of the exact number of wounds received by Christ in his Passion, said to be 5,490, according to a revelation of a pious woman recluse."[196]

According to Ross Dealy, the clearest and most articulated work that emphasizes the pain and suffering of Jesus is that of Bonaventure the Franciscan. He writes,

Bonaventure definitively articulated the theme [of the physical suffering of Jesus]. Subjected to excruciating physical pain, Christ is deformed by injury and bleeding. Among other tortures he is crowned with thorns; his hands and feet are pierced; he is pulled, stretched, and hurled to the ground. In *De perfectione vitae sorores (On the Perfection of life Addressed to Sisters)* Christ's sorrow resulting from his physical pains is directly related to the blood flowing from all parts of his body. "Indeed, no sorrow was comparable to yours...blood spans from five parts of your body: the hands and feet in the crucifixion, the head in the crowning of thorns, the whole body in the flagellation, and the heart in the opening of your side."[197]

---

[196] Ibid, 248. See also, Thomas H. Bestul, Texts of the Passion, Latin Devotional Literature and Medieval Society (Berlin, Boston: University of Pennsylvania Press), 68.

[197] Ross Dealy, The Stoic Origins of Erasmus' Philosophy of Christ, 249. See De perfectione vitae sorores 6.6. Opera omnia 8, p. 122, trans. Jose de vinck,

It was all about the cross. R. N. Swanson attests to this when he opines, "Response to the Passion is the key aspect of the late medieval western religion, so ubiquitous and so frequently encountered that it may even be overlooked as a commonplace. Commemoration of the Passion appears in virtually every art form, verbal or plastic. Such artistic manifestations have generally provided the core of considerations of 'Passion devotion.'"[198] Emphasis on the Passion of Christ led almost naturally to identification with the suffering Son of Mary, the child of Bethlehem.

3.4. Passion Devotions and Identification with the Suffering Christ

After the stigmata experience of St. Francis, there were no more doubts in the minds of people that Jesus became one of us so that we can share in his divinity. The way of sharing in that divinity tended to be identifying with the suffering Christ. With St. Francis, the humble and poor one mysteriously receiving the marks of the wounds of Christ, the medieval men and women understood that they needed, as maintained by St. Bonaventure, to either be or not be a branch of the mystical vine.[199]

> The goal, according to *Vitis mystica*, is to participate in Christ's suffering by impressing on our minds mental pictures of the event, seeing "with the eyes of mind"—words also used in his *Commentary on the Sentences*. Carrying the

---

Works of Bonaventure 1:243.

[198] R. N. Swanson, "Passion and Practice: The Social and Ecclesiastical Implications of the Passion Devotion in the Late Middle Ages," in The Broken Body: Passion Devotion in Late-Medieval Culture, ed. R. M. Schlusemann, Bernhard. Ridderbos, and A. A. MacDonald, Mediaevalia Groningana; 21 (Groningen: Egbert Forsten, 1998), (1–30), 1.

[199] Cf. Ross Dealy, The Stoic Origins of Erasmus' Philosophy of Christ, 250. Vitis mystica 4.1. Opera omnia 8, p. 166, trans. Jose de vinck, Works of Bonaventure 1:158.

theme a step further, we need to be like Jesus, deformed outwardly in our bodies in order to be reformed inwardly. Even the humanist Giovanni Pico della Mirandolla (1463–94) whipped himself in remembrance of Christ's Passion. Caroline Bynum has shown that in the late Middle Ages "imitations of Christ came to have a literal meaning." Catherine of Siena (d. 1380) "craved blood because she craved identification with the humanity of Christ, and she saw this humanity as physicality." Catherine of Genoa (d. 1510) "consciously and explicitly chose food as her central image for mystical union." Behind Eucharistic devotion was the belief (the doctrine of transubstantiation) that "One *became* Christ's crucified body in *eating* Christ's crucified body." Both priests and recipients were literally pregnant with Christ.[200]

The Middle Ages developed a spirituality centered on individual identification with Christ's Passion.[201] R. N. Swanson states,

[I]mitation need not go to the point of death; to suffer for Christ, to experience the humiliation of the Passion might be enough. "Take up thy cross" might well be interpreted literally, as with Juseanos who, Jean Gerson reported, were wondering about in Italy. Other physical humiliations could also be self-inflicted, through flagellation. Flagellation might then be more than merely penitential discipline (although that was

[200] Ibid, 249–250. Vitis mystica 4.1. Opera omnia 8, p. 166, trans. Jose de vinck, Works of Bonaventure 1:158. See also, Caroline Walker Bynum, Holy Feast and Holy Fast: The Religious Significance of Food to Medieval Women, Revised edition (Berkeley: University of California Press, 1988), 185–259.
[201] Cf. Ross Dealy, The Stoic Origins of Erasmus' Philosophy of Christ, 251.

probably its main function); it also becomes an experience matching part of Christ's physical experience—able on a much-reduced scale. Painful asceticism implied imitation, as in the case of the fifteenth-century Breton Franciscan, Jean Discalcéat, who "faisait de son existence toute entière une Passion, une identification au Christ, dans la ligne de Francois d' Assise." Other parallels could also be drawn, which did not demand physical suffering to count as imitation. Johannes von Staupitz thus urges the audience to his Lenten sermons of 1520 to imitate successive stages of the Passion narratives by adopting a parallel course. For the Arrest, therefore, "we must imitate Him [Christ] by suffering all things out of love for God and the neighbor."[202]

While for Johannes von Staupitz it seems only the stage of the arrest of Christ required imitation by love of God and the neighbor, for Margery Kempe and Julian of Norwich, union and identification with Christ at all levels was interpreted to be a demonstration of Christians' love for him (Christ) and for the world. Just as Jesus loved the world and became human for our sake, to identify with the suffering Lord was a sign of one's love for the world as well. Ellen M. Ross writes, "Christians' identification with the suffering Jesus functioned in the process of spiritual transformation to deepen believers' relationship with God and the world."[203] Even though our suffering is nothing compared to that of the historical Jesus, to suffer, whether physically or emotionally as Jesus did, was geared toward "a deep-

---

[202] R. N. Swanson, "Passion and Practice: The Social and Ecclesiastical Implications of the Passion Devotion in the Late Middle Ages," 16. For the original idea of Johannnes von Staupitz, see: Rudolf K. Markwald, A Mystic's Passion: The Spirituality of Johannes von Staupitz in his 1520 Lenten Sermons (NY: Peter Lang, 1990), 56–79.

[203] Ellen M. Ross, The Grief of God: Images of the Suffering Jesus in Late Medieval England, 31.

ening relationship of love and knowledge with the God of love."[204] Medieval Christians did "not seek a momentary ecstatic experience of God, nor did they write a disinterested ontological analysis of the divine life; rather, they envisioned a holistic lifelong path on which a growing relationship with the divine is coupled with a deepening love of self and neighbor."[205]

In the Church of the Middle Ages, there seemed to have been a gap between what theology expressed and stipulated and how people understood and lived their Christian lives. For the medieval Christian, soaked in a world that seemed to have been locked in a vicious circle of pain and suffering, identification with the suffering Christ was the faith response. To be a Christian simply meant to identify oneself with the suffering Christ. Loving identification with the crucified Lord might have been solidarity, through mortification, with the suffering people of God if one was not personally suffering. Or it could have been a peaceful and stress-free way to live a Christian life without struggling to find reasons to accept or reject the suffering against which one could do nothing. For if Christ, the Son of God suffered, who are we not to suffer? This Christian spirituality of iden-tification with the suffering Christ of the Middle Ages made its way through centuries and was certainly of great help and comfort to the masses. But with the changing conditions for improved way of life in the nineteenth and twentieth centuries, a Church that identified with the suffering Christ was more and more becoming—at least according to Schillebeeckx—irrelevant and unpopular.

---

[204] Ibid, 33.

[205] Cf. Ellen M. Ross, The Grief of God: Images of the Suffering Jesus in Late Medieval England, 33.

Chapter 4

The Message of the Cross in Edward Schillebeeckx's Theology: God Is Not Responsible for Our Suffering

The cross of Jesus, but also the cross (pains and sufferings) of the world from all ages, has been a persistent subject of studies and discussions. It is held that through his passion, death, and resurrection, Jesus achieved the salvation of the world. Most—and maybe all—theologians accept the vital importance of the resurrection as a definitive sign of God's endorsement of Jesus's lifestyle. They also interpret the resurrection to be God's way of vindicating, rendering justice to the unjust condemnation of Jesus. But the same theologians disagree on their interpretation of the cross. Was the cross an accidental event in the life of Jesus? Or was it part and parcel of the Father's plan for the Son? To directly state the matter, did the Father intend, right from the beginning, that the Son goes through such a brutal death for the salvation of the world? The answer provided to these questions also situates one's response to and understanding of pain and suffering in the world. For Edward Schillebeeckx, God was not responsible for the death of Jesus Christ. Humanity put Jesus on the cross. It is the human injustice that led to the condemnation and the subsequent crucifixion of Jesus. The implication of Schillebeeckx's understanding of the origin of the pain and suffering of Jesus is that God was not and is not the origin of either the cross of Jesus or the suffering of humanity as a whole or of each person. Our persistent question hence remains: If God is not the origin of the cross, who is?

4.1. Context of Schillebeeckx's Theological Excursus

We will not be able to understand Schillebeeckx's method of theologizing unless we try to know him and understand his context and the perspective from which he was doing theology. Born in Antwerp, Belgium, in 1914, Schillebeeckx died in 2009. Even though as a young man he went to the Jesuit school, he entered the Order of Preachers (OP). History recalls that Schillebeeckx, one of the great Dominican theologians of the twentieth century, was always intrigued by new problems. William Hill explains that the core of the Schillebeeckx' theological inquiry was the question of the mediation of the transcendent. The "epicenter [of his theology] is surely the question concerning the historical mediation of the transcendent—one that successfully avoids the Scylla of deism, on the one hand, and the the [sic] Charybdis of pantheism on the other."[206] In common man's language, Schillebeeckx was highly interested in God's self-communication to humanity through the prophets, Jesus, and the Church, and the way humanity understood and interpreted God. Do we know and understand God in the right way? If yes, then why does our proclamation about God and his Church seem unattractive to present generations?

4.1.1. Relevance of Jesus

The effort to make God and the Church relevant to a world engulfed in deism and pantheism was that which truly inspired Schillebeeckx. William Portier writes, "Like Rahner, Lonergan, and Tracy, Schillebeeckx has spent most of his life as a theological professor, a member of the professional elite in both the church and society. Strangely enough, however, he doesn't consider his primary public to

---

[206] William J. Hill, "Human Happiness as God's Honor: Background to a Theology in Transition," in The Praxis of Christian Experience: An Introduction to the Theology of Edward Schillebeeckx, eds. Robert J. Schreiter and Mary Catherine Hilkert, 1st ed (S.F: Harper & Row, 1989), 7.

be the academy. Nor is his intended public narrowly ecclesiastical."[207] In his book *Jesus an Experiment in Christology*, Schillebeeckx affirms,

> Although I regard this book as a Christian interpretation of Jesus—a Christology, however unconventional it may be—it was not written to resolve the sometimes very subtle problems that interest the academic theologian. Not that these are unimportant. But the fact is that believers are raising questions about Christ which are not ones that normally preoccupy academics. I have tried to bridge the gap between academic theology and the concrete needs of ordinary Christians or, more modestly, to shed some light on the nexus of problems presaging that gap and giving rise to the questions that seem most urgent to ordinary Christians.[208]

While Schillebeeckx was very concerned about the questions asked by an ordinary Christian of his time, he remained committed to understanding and projecting Jesus as well as the Church as credible and relevant to modern and somewhat secular men and women. The relevance of Jesus is rooted in how his (Jesus's) contemporaries understood him, that is, as a savior. Salvation, for the contemporaries of Jesus, was not merely a religious concept, it also had a day-to-day, living ramifications. In fact, Schillebeeckx demonstrates,

> Ideas and expectations of salvation and human happiness are invariably projected from within

---

[207] William Portier, "Interpretation and Method" in The Praxis of Christian Experience: An Introduction to the Theology of Edward Schillebeeckx, eds. Robert J. Schreiter and Mary Catherine Hilkert, 1st ed (S.F: Harper & Row, 1989), 21.

[208] Edward Schillebeeckx, The Collected Works of Edward Schillebeeckx Volume 6: Jesus: An Experiment in Christology, (London: T&T Clark, 2014). Kindle Edition, loc. 417.

concrete experience and the pondered fact of calamity, pain, misery and alienation—from within negative experiences accumulated through centuries of affliction, with here and there the fleeting promise of a happier lot, fragmentary experiences of well-being in a story, stretching from generation to generation, of hopes unfulfilled, of guilt and evil: the "Job's problem" of human history. Hence there eventually emerges an anthropological projection, a vision of what is held to be the true, good and happy mode of human life. This is why the human craving for happiness and well-being, always being submitted to critical judgement yet again and again surviving every critique, inevitably acquires—in diverse forms—the pregnant nuance of "release from" or "deliverance out of" and, at the same time, of entering into a "completely new world."[209]

The Jews—specifically the population living at the time of Jesus—expected to be released from and be delivered from evil, poverty, sickness, pains, miseries, and alienation, etc. The situation was so dire that they lived only hoping for better days. It is no wonder Schillebeeckx asserts,

[F]or both Jew and gentile, Jesus' time was full to bursting with an assortment of hopes regarding some good thing to come, in the form of a welter of ideas culled from long centuries of fleeting promise and, more especially, of many unfulfilled expectations. The period of Jewish apocalypticism above all, from the Maccabean struggle (167 BC) and the Jewish War (AD 66–70) to Bar Kochba (AD 135), was a "story of blood and

---

[209] Ibid, loc. 490–497.

tears," from which the yearning grew: "Enough is enough: the world must be changed—positively and radically changed!"[210]

Jesus embodied the change expected by the people. We shall return to this claim when we discuss Jesus's public ministry and his proclamation of the kingdom of God. Here, it suffices to simply state that vis-à-vis Jesus, "History shows [...] a story of people who found salvation, explicitly qualified as 'from God', in Jesus of Nazareth, whom they came to describe—when faced in the context of their expectant hope with this concrete historical manifestation—as 'the Christ, son of God, our Lord.'"[211]

Schillebeeckx is not naive. He acknowledges that the salvation (the good-to-come) may in the world take different forms, depending on both the culture in which one finds self and the understanding that one has of a fulfilled way of life. "Our hopes of good-to-come have a different complexion and focus. Our conceptions of that good are different too."[212] And he continues, "All ways of envisaging 'salvation' and all hopes regarding man's 'true mode of existence' are in any case culturally conditioned."[213] But for Schillebeeckx, if modern people ever yearned for a world free of pain, suffering, poverty, misery, and alienation, then Jesus can play a role in this world, just as he did play a role in the lives of the poor and marginalized, the rejected and sick, the religious and nonreligious people of his time. That some were still facing diseases, alienations, rejection, and were in search of a savior or saving methods for a better way of life in the twentieth century was quite evident for Schillebeeckx. He, for instance, writes,

> All along our experience has been that even out of our catastrophic Western history a utopia is growing among us. This concrete experience has been reflected in all sorts of emancipatory

---

[210] Ibid, loc. 508–516.
[211] Ibid, loc. 490.
[212] Ibid, loc. 551.
[213] Ibid, loc. 556.

movements—movements intended to deliver people from their social alienation, while various scientific techniques (psychotherapeutic release; Gestalt therapy; androgogy; social work; counseling, etc.) were meant to free them from the loss of personal identity. In our day the existence of a number of factors in our lives, [...] to induce well-being and to heal people or make them whole, has forced itself on our awareness more than ever before. This puts the statement—till recently bandied about in some Christian circles without the slightest reservation—that "all true salvation comes from Jesus Christ alone," in a problematic, thoroughly opaque, at the very least astounding context of implausibility.[214]

Since God's self-disclosure is not a mere occurrence of the past but a continuing phenomenon,[215] Schillebeeckx seems to suggest that we need to rediscover or reinterpret Jesus and his offer of salvation within the actual context of the modern and postmodern world.

4.1.2. Relevance of the Church

Schillebeeckx also maintains the importance of the Church. "As a hermeneutic of history and of Christian praxis, Schillebeeckx's theology views Christianity not as a privileged segment of the universal history, namely, the chronicle of God's dealing with humanity through Israel and the Christ event, but of all of history seen from the vantage point of God himself as the Lord of history, as the one who ultimately gives meaning to history."[216] Through Israel, the Christ event, and now the Church, God impacted and still influences not only history but the world too in a definitive way. It is through the

---

[214] Ibid, loc. 585–592.
[215] Cf. William J. Hill, "Human Happiness as God's Honor: Background to a Theology in Transition," 9.
[216] Ibid, 7.

ekklesia that Jesus, and his liberating actions and saving events, has been made known and is part of the world.

> The gospels tell us what Jesus came to mean to a group of people known eventually as the *ekklesia* of Christ. The early writings of this community, collated in the New Testament to be read, meditated upon and studied as their book, are still today, for all conscious members of this "Christ movement," a source of critical reflection on their life and conduct as Christians. At the same time Jesus' concretization in literature, namely in that same New Testament, has given him form and substance. He is, as it were, objectivized in it. This puts him right in the limelight in a special way. Thanks to the transmitted documents Jesus is part of world literature and has become accessible to all. He has become "common property"; and the New Testament is not just the exclusive book of Christendom.[217]

In a deduction, Schillebeeckx is underlining the significance of the Church in keeping Jesus alive—both in religious and nonreligious milieux—through the centuries. The instrumentality of the Church as God's means of giving meaning and sense to history does not make her (the Church) an island in the world. Instead, while she articulates her idea of salvation, the Church needs also to listen to the world. The importance of the Church is not an objective one, but an importance in relation. Commenting on Schillebeeckx understanding of the role of the Church in the world, Susan A. Ross remarks,

> Insofar as the church is a social and historical reality, it is open to criticism on both historical and

---

[217] Edward Schillebeeckx, The Collected Works of Edward Schillebeeckx Volume 6: Jesus: An Experiment in Christology, loc. 641–647.

theological grounds. Therefore Schillebeeckx sees the role of the theologian as continually reminding and confronting the church to be conscious of its own interests: the community of believers in the service of the message of Jesus. This means that new situations can and do give rise to new expressions, on the ongoing faith of the church. These new expressions, however, inevitably collide with the human reality of the church, and the established order of the church—a historical reality—can become rigid and resistant to change. Indeed, this rigidity can and in fact has, over the course of the church history, "become fixed as an ideology and itself hinders the original purpose of the church."[218]

The ability of the Church to enter into a conversation with the secular world, to listen to our experiences and what others (non-Christians) have to say about Jesus and salvation will go a long way to asserting, not only her importance, but also her credibility. Consequently, the question becomes, "What are our new experiences, and what is the world saying? What is the world's experience of well-being, the good to come; and what is its understanding of the narrative of Jesus's life?" Schillebeeckx is particularly interested in these questions, but most importantly in the "new experiences [that] have an 'authority' as they reveal our liberation from oppressive structures even within the church."[219]

"In spite of radical pluralism and disagreement about what constitutes humanity and human happiness, Schillebeeckx remarks that we know, in at least a negative way, what violates humanity. Situations of evil and injustice trigger the spontaneous response: 'No,

---

[218] Susan A. Ross, "Salvation in and for the World: Church and Sacraments," in The Praxis of Christian Experience: An Introduction to the Theology of Edward Schillebeeckx, eds. Robert J. Schreiter and Mary Catherine Hilkert, 1st ed (S.F: Harper & Row, 1989), 108.

[219] Ibid, 109.

it can't go like this, we won't stand for it any longer.'"[220] Human instinctive reaction to suffering is rejection and resistance. Therefore, if the Church, the historical body of Christ, intends to be relevant and credible to the then twentieth—and today's twenty-first—century men and women, then it can't be a Church that identifies with pain and suffering. In the previous chapter, I have largely explained how the suffering and crucified Lord was placed at the center of the medieval Christian practices. To be a saint, to claim to be a genuine Christian who truly loved God and the neighbor, meant to be able to identify with the suffering Lord—by either accepting or, in some cases, looking for suffering (self-mortification). Within the new context of the world, Schillebeeckx believed that the Church must act like Jesus did more than two thousand years ago by denouncing, rejecting, and fighting any inhuman (evil, suffering, pain, and oppression) thing that humankind faces. Such actions if taken by the Church, besides agreeing with Jesus's revelation of God, will not be different from the experience of the instinctive human reaction when faced with suffering and pain.

4.2. Experience and Contrast Experience

In chapter 1, I established how the exilic and post-exilic periods informed the way people perceived and understood God. These experiences led—in some strains of the Old Testament—to the belief that God is the source of pain and suffering. For Thomas Aquinas, as seen in chapter 2, God could be identified as the cause of evil in as much as he permits it either for the common good, or in respect to human freedom. In a very astute way, Schillebeeckx does not deny or repudiate Old Testament formulations of God. Rather he explains that our ancestors, both of the Old Testament and those of the Middle Ages, missed an important element about their experience, which Schillebeeckx names "contrast experience." But Schillebeeckx also

---

[220] Mary Catherine Hilkert, "The Discovery of the Living God: Revelation and Experience," in The Praxis of Christian Experience: An Introduction to the Theology of Edward Schillebeeckx, eds. Robert J. Schreiter and Mary Catherine Hilkert, 1st ed (S.F: Harper & Row, 1989), 41.

wants to pay attention to present-day experiences as mediating the transcendent. Maybe the most telling explanation of such a theological orientation is that "[t]he very history of experiences that forms one's interpretative horizon also serves to keep one open to new experiences. Truly experienced persons, Schillebeeckx notes, are the most open to new dimensions of reality as they integrate new moments of experience into an expanding sphere of reference."[221] Schillebeeckx perceives and understands Christ's message within such an extended context of the expectations of both Jesus's contemporaries and twentieth-century people. J. B. Webster explains that for Schillebeeckx,

> the field of reference of Christology is wider than that of Jesus' past: it also includes our present interaction with him. And so "the life of Christians in the world in which they live is a fifth gospel: it also belongs to the heart of Christology." Above all this is because Jesus Christ is present, his story as it were unfinished as his salvation extends into the world. Thus we do not need to choose between faithfulness to the past and openness to the present, or between an objective Christology and a subjective account of human experience, precisely because of who Jesus Christ is: the living one in whom salvation is to be found.[222]

In his early writings, Schillebeeckx maintained that "the traces of the living God who is 'the future of humanity' can be discovered in human experience—even in experiences of radical suffering."[223] His later writings, however, disclose the concept of a God who is revealed

---

[221] Ibid, 37.

[222] John B. Webster "Edward Schillebeeckx: God is 'Always Absolutely New.'" Evangel: A Quarterly Review of Biblical, Practical and Contemporary Theology, (Autumn 1984) 5–10, 8.

[223] Mary Catherine Hilkert, "The Discovery of the Living God: Revelation and Experience," 35.

in human experience, but in a dialectical, rather than direct fashion.[224] If the entirety of human experience is to be identical to direct divine revelation, then one could easily blame God for all the troubles (pain, suffering, and evils) of this world. Schillebeeckx believes that our Christian experience and understanding of God is not one of suffering, pain, and oppression, etc., but that of salvation, that is, wholeness and wellness of humanity.[225] Therefore, "What Christians say about God and Christ should be related to the human quest for meaning and liberation in a world where there is a surplus of suffering. The experience of salvation from God in Christ must always be connected with human flourishing, which entails the overcoming of evil and suffering."[226]

As already pointed out, Schillebeeckx unequivocally suggests that human beings instinctively reject or react negatively to pain and suffering. "No, it can't go like this, we won't stand for it any longer,"[227] we say. Borderline, negative and painful experiences, or to use Schillebeeckx's expression, "contrast experience," dialectically understood from the perspective of the human reactions to them, make us realize God's opposition to them. In a nutshell, Schillebeeckx suggests that our collective and individual experience of God is that of the God who wills the wholeness and the happiness of humanity. But we understand or know this through a dialectical interpretation of our daily "contrast experiences" and an appropriation of our positive experiences. God cannot be understood from outside of human experience. And if human beings instinctively oppose evil, the God who created us in his image and likeness cannot be different.

Schillebeeckx focuses on the contrast experience as the point of departure for the reinterpretation of God's interaction with humanity. Instead of moving from the doctrines or dogmatic elaboration of

---

[224] Ibid, 36.

[225] Cf. Mary Catherine Hilkert, "The Discovery of the Living God: Revelation and Experience," 36.

[226] Robin Ryan, God and the Mystery of Human Suffering: A Theological Conversation Across the Ages (NY: Paulist Press, 2011), 221.

[227] Mary Catherine Hilkert, "The Discovery of the Living God: Revelation and Experience," 41.

the Church to the understanding or formulating of language about God, he turns to narrative. This narrative must at the same time be faithful to our human experiences, our interpretation of reality and expression of those truths. In a sense, for Schillebeeckx, experience in general, but contrast experience in particular, should be the leading factor in the interpretation of our collective experience of God's interaction with the world. From the interpreted experience, we will finally be able to unlock our expressions or discourses about God—that will always remain limited. Because our human expressions or formulations of the divine reality always fall short of the entire fact of God, the narration of every experience can—and must not—lead to a refreshed, renewed understanding or experience of our tradition.

> Schillebeeckx concludes that human experience has a narrative structure. One who has had an experience with some power to disclose reality (an authoritative experience) spontaneously wants to express what has happened. Experience is communicated primarily through words—we share our experience by telling stories. Traditions, formed from collective experience, become the social framework for understanding—the common stories of families, communities, and cultures. Narration opens up the possibility of sharing in a new story. Through narration, one is able to offer others the possibility of a new "experience with experiences."[228]

It seems that for our Flemish theologian, the more experiences and narratives we have, the better we are in our approach and understanding of the divine reality. For insight into the character of God develops through history. From this perspective, John Webster notes, "In an interview Schillebeeckx once said that God is always absolutely new. He is never exhausted. Certainly never in the kingdom

---

[228] Ibid, 39.

which he establishes among us. There is always openness. We have to leave God his freedom in being new with regard to us [...] God is new each day. He is a constant source of new possibilities... He is always surprising us."[229]

At this juncture, we need to establish a couple of things: (1) For very good experiential and theological reasons, God was considered the source of pain and suffering. (2) Because our formulations of God remain limited and, he is always new in regard to us, we still have a long way to go in our knowledge of him. (3) Today, for similarly good experiential reasons, we can't find any reason for evil, pain, and suffering in God.

4.3. Schillebeeckx's Theology of Suffering

There is the reality of pain and suffering in the world. But no one, no generation wants to be associated with it. Schillebeeckx starts by agreeing with traditional knowledge or theology that not all suffering is meaningless. "Not all suffering is meaningless. That is part of the sum of human wisdom, as the whole of human history bears witness."[230] Suffering may help people to grow and mature in goodness, and in compassion. We may all recall expressions such as, "I learned my lesson the hard way." This suggests that we were able to achieve or know something about life, God, or reality through pain and suffering. It is no surprise, "[i]n almost all languages, people rightly speak of a 'school of suffering.' In our human world, great things are evidently born only in suffering."[231] A person can also willingly accept suffering as a sign of commitment and responsibility for something dear to his/her heart. Schillebeeckx makes sure to explain that in this case suffering is neither sought nor created.[232] However,

---

[229] John B. Webster "Edward Schillebeeckx: God Is 'Always Absolutely New,'" 8.

[230] Edward Schillebeeckx, Christ, the Experience of Jesus as Lord (NY: Seabury Press, 1980), 724.

[231] Ibid, 724.

[232] Cf. Edward Schillebeeckx, Christ, the Experience of Jesus as Lord, 725.

it is accepted as a possible consequence of a commitment to a particular project.[233]

Second, Schillebeeckx rejects the connection that has always been made between sin and suffering / suffering and sin. He asserts, "Jesus breaks with the idea that suffering has necessarily something to do with sinfulness."[234] To support his comments, Schillebeeckx leans on two different passages. When Jesus was asked who sinned in the case of the man born blind in John's Gospel, Jesus replied, "Neither he nor his parents" (John 9:2). While commenting on the fate of those Galileans who were murdered by Pilate, Jesus maintained, "Do you think that these Galileans were worse sinners than all the other Galileans, because they suffered in this way?" (Luke 13:2). For Schillebeeckx, sin could somehow lead to suffering. But to think that all suffering is the result of sin can be misleading. He writes, "It is possible to draw conclusions from sin to suffering, but not from suffering to sin."[235] He goes ahead to suggest that if sin should lead to suffering, then there must be an opportunity for repentance. Any suffering that does not lead to conversion is something that God opposes and is concerned to remove.[236]

Even though Schillebeeckx has already identified that suffering does not necessarily mean sin, he has also shown that any pain without opportunity for conversion is unacceptable, meaningless. It is this extreme suffering in the world that sets Schillebeeckx on edge. "[D]oes someone perhaps wants to give Buchenwald, Auschwitz, or Vietnam [or whatever else] a specific structural place in the divine plan?"[237] he asked. In other words, did the suffering, death of those men, women, and children in the concentration camps and in countries devastated by war give them any chance to repent? Can we provide any evidence that these people needed to repent from any sin whatsoever? While we cannot know with certitude if the pain and suffering provided an opportunity for repentance or not,

---

[233] Ibid.
[234] Ibid, 695.
[235] Ibid.
[236] Cf. Edward Schillebeeckx, Christ, the Experience of Jesus as Lord, 695.
[237] Ibid, 725.

because "of course we are not God,"[238] we can ascertain one fact. For Schillebeeckx, besides the cruel nature of what people went through in concentration camps and war zones, all these men and women suffered innocently. And if we consider suffering and pains as such, it is not too different from our neighbors' or our own innocent suffering. This suffering that as human beings we react negatively to and reject cannot be given any meaning. Accordingly, Schillebeeckx states, "Human reason cannot, in fact, cope with the concentrated historical suffering and evil. Here the human Logos, human rationality fails: it cannot give any explanation."[239]

The meaninglessness of the suffering of the innocent, the automatic human rejection of it, according to Schillebeeckx, suggests something fundamental about God and his plan for humanity. If we cannot justify evil, and the unfathomable mass of innocent suffering, or explain it as being significantly unavoidable in the realization of God's fundamental plan and his will for good, then we cannot look for or find the ground of suffering in God, even though suffering brings the believer directly up against God.[240] Schillebeeckx suggests that in God there is no negativity. He writes, "God is pure positivity, he wills the life of the sinner and not his death."[241] But can we find a ground for evil in God, in case we can explain it as being necessary for his will for good? The absolute positivity of God, Schillebeeckx objects, also suggests his outright rejection of or opposition to evil. To make his opinion clear, Schillebeeckx reinforces his argument by suggesting that God must be both pure positivity and against evil. We must also recognize, he stipulates, that "God" by being pure positivity, the "first principle" of good he (God) is simultaneously in no way the ground of any evil. Simply stated, God is the author of the good and the opponent of evil.[242] Though God's sovereignty, the painful experiences, and a strong anti-dualism instigated some of the Old Testament writers to make provision for pain and suffering in

---

[238] Ibid, 725.

[239] Ibid, 726.

[240] Cf. Edward Schillebeeckx, Christ, the Experience of Jesus as Lord, 726.

[241] Ibid, 727.

[242] Cf. Edward Schillebeeckx, Christ, the Experience of Jesus as Lord, 727.

God, Schillebeeckx suggests that God's ultimate revelation in Jesus discloses his opposition to evil. The God of Jesus "transcends [...] negative aspects of our history, not so much by *allowing them*, as *by overcoming them*, making them as though they had not happened."[243] We can now turn to how Schillebeeckx understands and interprets the life and mission of Christ.

4.3.1. Retelling the Story of Jesus

"Schillebeeckx's Christology *begins with a problem, and not a formula or a theory.* His quest for a suitable starting point common to all human life and therefore accessible to all, leads him to concentrate on the universal experience of evil, the bitter awareness that the history of human race is a history of suffering."[244] Schillebeeckx establishes two significant axes of interpretation of Jesus's life and salvific mission.

4.3.1.1. The Public Ministry of Jesus

He notes, "First, of all, the good news is for the poor. Strikingly, the signs for the coming of the kingdom and God's righteousness [Matthew 6:33], in the coming of the Messiah ['the one who is to come'], [Matthew 11:3] are: the blind see, the lame walk, the lepers are cleansed, and the deaf hear, the dead are raised, and the poor have the good news preached to them [Matthew 11:4ff]."[245] God's first action through Jesus is to alleviate, to oppose, to utterly destroy, and to annihilate all negative power that keeps humanity in its grips. While according to some Old Testament passages the coming of the Messiah was about the painful annihilation of sinful humanity, in

---

[243] Ibid, 729, with added emphasis.

[244] John P. Galvin, "Retelling the Story of Jesus: Christology," in The Praxis of Christian Experience: An Introduction to the Theology of Edward Schillebeeckx, eds. Robert J. Schreiter and Mary Catherine Hilkert, 1st ed (SF: Harper & Row, 1989), 53–54, with added emphasis.

[245] Edward Schillebeeckx, Christ, the Experience of Jesus as Lord, 695.

Jesus God declares or unleashes his annihilating battle against evil and suffering.

The second overarching axis of Schillebeeckx's reinterpretative effort is the kingdom of God. Like most scholars, Schillebeeckx believes that Jesus's life, ministry, death, and resurrection revolved around the establishment of the kingdom of God. Pope Benedict the XVI in his second book on Jesus of Nazareth entitled *Jesus of Nazareth: From the Baptism in the Jordan to the Transfiguration* gives a statistical report of the usage of the expression the kingdom of God. He writes, "A look at the statistics underscores this. The Phrase, the 'Kingdom of God,' occurs 122 times in the New Testament as a whole: 99 of these passages are found in the three synoptic Gospels, and 90 of these 99 texts report words of Jesus."[246] Robin Ryan remarked that "when asked by an interviewer about the 'keyword' in the story of Jesus, Schillebeeckx answered 'the kingdom.' [And Ryan continues] 'Jesus,' he says, 'offered no precise definition of the kingdom of God.'"[247] For throughout his public ministry, Jesus "talked of a mysterious new future: it was called the kingdom of God. This was a new happy life, a kingdom for the poor fishermen, joy for those who weep, fullness for those who are hungry."[248] Unlike John the Baptist and most of the Old Testament prophets, the mysterious kingdom proclaimed by Jesus was neither cast into an absolute future nor in an aeon different from this one. Jesus's futuristic life-giving kingdom was subtly already breaking in, in the here and now. Schillebeeckx points out,

> *Basileia tou Theou* is the kingdom of God, God's lordship, the realm of God. It does not denote a sovereign realm above and beyond this world, where God supposedly resides and reigns. What Jesus means by it is an event in which God begins

---

[246] Joseph Ratzinger, Jesus of Nazareth: From the Baptism in the Jordan to the Transfiguration, 1st ed. (NY: Doubleday, 2007), 47.

[247] Robin Ryan, God and the Mystery of Human Suffering, 22.

[248] Edward Schillebeeckx, God Among Us: The Gospel Proclaimed (NY: Crossroad Pub., 1983), 175.

to govern and act as king or Lord, hence an act in which God manifests his Godhead in the human world. Thus God's lordship or dominion is the divine power itself in its saving acts in our history, and at the same time the final, eschatological state that brings to an end the evil world, dominated by the forces of calamity and woe, and initiates the new world in which God "comes into his own": "your kingdom come." (Mt. 6: 10)[249]

In Jesus, God's concern for humanity, for a fully alive humanity was revealed. For Schillebeeckx, that means that in Jesus, the true nature of God who does not want and does not delight in the suffering of humanity was revealed. If the Old Testament and John the Baptist understood the approaching judgment as filled with pain and suffering, Jesus has an entirely different perspective. For him (Jesus) the impending judgment that will inaugurate the kingdom will be a demonstration of God's compassionate and unconditional will, God's desire to save his people. The

"expectation of the end" is an expectation of the approaching kingdom of God. And for Jesus this means the closeness of God's unconditional will to salvation, of compassionate outreach and proffered mercy and, along with this, opposition to all forms of evil: suffering and sin.[250]

In Jesus's proclamation, the kingdom to come is not in some absolute future, but in the future, that is already present in the moment. The future is with God, as "a God of men"[251] who opposes evil, but saves and liberates humanity in the here and now. How do we know that?

---

[249] Edward Schillebeeckx, The Collected Works of Edward Schillebeeckx Volume 6: Jesus: An Experiment in Christology, loc. 3178–3184.
[250] Ibid, loc. 3156–3159.
[251] Ibid, loc. 3203.

Schillebeeckx observes that "Jesus is a parable."[252] He is both the parable of God, but also the parable of the kingdom that he proclaimed. For this reason, Schillebeeckx suggests that to understand Jesus's message of the kingdom and know the God that he proclaims throughout his life we need, as we go through the Gospels, to ask one simple question. "What are these gospels really trying to tell us when they report, for instance, the miracles of Jesus?"[253] First, the Gospels tell us that Jesus has introduced a new logic in the world. It is a logic of "a new world in which only grace and love can dwell, and which places under judgment and seeks to change our history of human suffering, the outcome of our short-sighted behavior."[254] Second, in Jesus's lifestyle, parables, and teachings, we are confronted with "God's saving activity [...]; this is how God acts, and it is to be seen in the actions of Jesus."[255]

Consequently, the questions "whether Jesus brought salvation or harbored 'a demon,'"[256] or, "whether Jesus was a bringer of good or ill,"[257] asked by his contemporaries were uncalled for. "The message of the kingdom of God that Jesus preached and embodied in his behavior reflects a God whose concern is the concern of humankind, whose coming rule means life and wholeness for people."[258] Jesus healed the sick: lepers (see Matthew 8:1–4, Mark 1:40–45, Luke 5:12–15) and blind men (Matthew 9:27–31, John 9:1–12). And he liberated people from evil spirits' possession (Matthew 8:28–34, Mark 5:1–15, Luke 8:26–39). About the New Testament stories of the healing and exorcism activities of Jesus, "Schillebeeckx contends that though the miracle tradition was expanded in Christian reflection of the life of Jesus, there is a historically firm basis for affirming that Jesus acted as both a healer and an exorcist."[259] Jesus did not only

---

[252] Ibid, loc. 3499.
[253] Ibid, loc. 3495.
[254] Ibid, loc. 3432–3534.
[255] Ibid, loc. 3526.
[256] Ibid, loc. 6933.
[257] Ibid, loc. 6943.
[258] Robin Ryan, God and the Mystery of Human Suffering, 224.
[259] Ibid, 225.

heal and perform exorcisms, he also fed the poor (see Mark 6:30–44, Matthew 14:13–21, Luke 9:10–17, John 6:1–15) and had a table fellowship with all kinds of people, including those who were considered disreputable by the religious and civic leaders as his way of disclosing and establishing God's kingdom.[260] In conclusion, through Jesus's activities and parables, we realize one single thing: God hates the pain and the suffering of humanity and will do all it takes to alleviate or remove their burden on humanity. Jesus's "God is a God who looks after people."[261] In short, for Jesus, a happy person makes a happy God. For "we are each other's happiness."[262] But a question remains: How does Schillebeeckx interpret the suffering of the coming one, identified in the Christian tradition as the Son of God?

4.3.1.2. The Death of Jesus

As for the suffering and death of Christ, Schillebeeckx does not restrain his thoughts. He disagrees with the classical theology that seems to maintain that God the Father put his Son on the cross for the expiation of the sins of the world. Such a theological perspective, he claims, gives a positive significance to suffering in all its forms.

> Thus, suffering and death become "a divine necessity" without which reconciliation is impossible. The various pictures which we find hinted at briefly in the New Testament, without any theorizing, later become a thought-out, rational system. This both weakens and "tames" the critical forces of the crucifixion of Jesus. Suffering as suffering (in whatever way) takes on a positive theological significance. God's honor, as theolo-

---

[260] Cf. Robin Ryan, God and the Mystery of Human Suffering, 224–225.

[261] Edward Schillebeeckx, The Collected Works of Edward Schillebeeckx Volume 6: Jesus: An Experiment in Christology, loc. 3206.

[262] Ibid, loc. 3201.

gians imagine this honor, is avenged through the suffering and blood.[263]

Referring to Thomas Aquinas, who thought that "it is a senseless philosophical undertaking to look for a particular cause, a ground or motive for evil and suffering in God,"[264] Schillebeeckx maintains God's innocence. "Negativity cannot have a cause or a motive in God.... [I]n that case, we cannot look for a divine reason for the death of Jesus either."[265] If God is not the cause or the reason for the suffering and death of Jesus, his Son, then who, or what is?

For Schillebeeckx, humanity bears the responsibility of the death of Jesus. He writes,

> God, who according to Leviticus "abominates human sacrifice" (Lev. 18:21–30; 20:1–5), did not put Jesus on the cross. Human beings did that. Although God always comes in power, divine power knows no use of force, not even against people who are crucifying his Christ.[266]

Schillebeeckx establishes that Jesus's message met with some opposition. And his failure to persuade the religious, and to some extent the political, leadership was the reason of his crucifixion. He says this:

> Jesus rejected both the Aramaic-Pharisaic exposition of the Law and the overbearing cultic devoutness of the Sadducees. His preaching and praxis struck at the very heart of the Judaic principle of "performance" in the religious sphere. In particular his solidarity with the "unclean" and

---

[263] Edward Schillebeeckx, Christ, the Experience of Jesus as Lord, 700.
[264] Ibid, 728.
[265] Ibid, 729.
[266] Edward Schillebeeckx, Church: The Human Story of God, trans. John Bowden (NY: Crossroad, 1993), 120–121.

with tax collectors and sinners was a thorn in the
flesh of pious officialdom—it was contrary to
"the Law."[267]

In rejecting some of the religious practices of his time, in having an open table fellowship with the "sinners," Jesus offended and
upset the leadership. Because he hurt them, they rejected him and his
message. He consequently became the rejected one. The rejection of
Jesus and his message was not only by religious officials or individual people, but also by entire cities such as Chorazin, Capernaum,
Bethsaida.[268] Faced with failure and rejection in Galilee and its sur-
rounding cities, Jesus headed to Jerusalem. The real motivation of
Jesus's decision to go to Jerusalem may never be known. Did he go to
Jerusalem because he felt he would be successful over there? Did he
go to suffer and die because "no prophet can die outside of Jerusalem"
(see Luke 13:31)? Did he go to bring his mission to Jerusalem as the
inevitable endpoint of his God-given mission? Or maybe simply to
get away from Galilee where he failed? For Schillebeeckx, whatever
the motivations of Jesus were, his movement toward Jerusalem was
due to failure and rejection. As if his failure outside Jerusalem was
not enough, in Jerusalem, Jesus performed the so-called purification
of the temple that led more or less immediately to his condemnation. But for Schillebeeckx, "even before Good Friday, Jesus was 'the
rejected one' and felt himself to be so on the basis of the historically
brief period of his public ministry."[269]

In Schillebeeckx's understanding, Jesus's failure to convince,
and people's rejection of his message, was the reason they killed him.
God did not wish the death of his Son in reparation for the sins of
the world. Instead, humanity refusing God's message proclaimed by

[267] Edward Schillebeeckx, The Collected Works of Edward Schillebeeckx Volume 6: Jesus: An Experiment in Christology, loc. 6936–6941.
[268] Cf. Edward Schillebeeckx, The Collected Works of Edward Schillebeeckx Volume 6: Jesus: An Experiment in Christology, loc. 6962.
[269] Ibid, loc. 7009–7013.

the Son, decided to violently—as a deterrent to others—silence him by killing him.[270]

The difference though is that the Son did not just allow the certainty of his death to take possession of him in an uncomprehending manner.[271] Rather, in a complete radical trust and by the grace of God, he (the Son) came to see in this historical situation some divine plan of salvation. In this perspective, Jesus came to the understanding that not only in spite of, but perhaps through the very failure within the history of his message, through his death, his message would be vindicated divinely and in sovereign freedom.[272] Once again Schillebeeckx wants his reader to understand that while God is not the reason for the impending suffering of the Son, the Son might have been forced by the circumstances to give not only a place, but also meaning to his approaching death in radical confidence in God.[273] From this perspective, he asserts that "we are not redeemed thanks to the death of Jesus but despite it."[274] Despite such violent, horrendous attitude of humanity toward God's Son, the Father and his Son still found a way—through the Son's faithfulness and the Father's acceptance or approval of it—to achieve the very purpose for which the Son was sent into the world: salvation. Robin Ryan remarks, "Some commentators stop here and conclude that this statement contains, in a nutshell, Schillebeeckx' understanding

---

[270] Jon Sobrino has a similar idea. He says, "Jesus was essentially a man in conflict, and because of this he was persecuted. This man in conflict got in the way, and in the simple words of Archbishop Romero, 'Those who get in the way get killed.' Jesus surrounded by conflict, got in the way, in the las resort because he got in the way of the other gods and got in the way in the name of God," he was killed. See Jon Sobrino, Christ the Liberator: A View from the Victims, (Maryknoll, NY: Orbis Books, 2001), 196.

[271] Cf. Edward Schillebeeckx, The Collected Works of Edward Schillebeeckx Volume 6: Jesus: An Experiment in Christology, loc. 7103.

[272] Cf. Edward Schillebeeckx, The Collected Works of Edward Schillebeeckx Volume 6: Jesus: An Experiment in Christology, loc. 7103.

[273] Cf. Edward Schillebeeckx, The Collected Works of Edward Schillebeeckx Volume 6: Jesus: An Experiment in Christology, loc. 7103–7107.

[274] Edward Schillebeeckx, Christ, the Experience of Jesus as Lord, 729.

of death in general and of the death of Jesus in particular."[275] But an attentive reader of Schillebeeckx should not miss that he says,

> [T]his "despite" is so transcended by God, not because he permits it in condescension but because through the resurrection of Jesus from the dead he conquers suffering and evil and undoes them, that the expression "despite the death" in fact does not say enough. However, the term in which we could fill this unfathomable "does not say enough" in a positive way, with finite, meaningful categories, escape us. What this "does not say enough" might suggest is expressed most clearly in the refusal of Jesus to look for a *culprit*. When the Jews ask, "Rabbi, who has sinned, this man or his parents, that he was born blind?" according to John 9:3 Jesus replied: "*Neither he nor his parents have sinned, but the works of God must be made manifest in him.*" God overcomes the initiative of what "finitude" can do purely of itself, without God's help—bringing suffering and evil into our history.[276]

In summary, God can always transform tragic events, engendered by human weakness and/or wickedness, into salvific realities.

4.3.1.3. The Resurrection of Jesus

The resurrection of Jesus is an act of God who detests evil. Through the resurrection of Jesus, God shows once again his abhorrence toward evil and his intention to bring something right out of tragedy. When humanity misjudges, when the devil strikes and inflicts pain and suffering, God rectifies and brings life and happi-

---

[275] Robin Ryan, God and the Mystery of Human Suffering, 231.
[276] Edward Schillebeeckx, Christ, the Experience of Jesus as Lord, 729–730.

ness. It is from this perspective that the resurrection of Christ must be understood.

Schillebeeckx deploys a lot of exegetical skill to demonstrate that the idea that Jesus raised himself from the dead was a later (second century) formulation. He writes, "Thus there seems to have been a tradition in early Christianity—the son of man tradition—which speaks quite clearly of Jesus rising. This tradition is evident only in John 10:17–18, where Jesus takes his life back on his own authority; somewhat later Ignatius of Antioch spelled this out emphatically, and the formula became classical in Christianity from the 2nd century onwards."[277] For Schillebeeckx, initially, the resurrection of Jesus was believed to be an act of God. The God of Jesus, who dislikes human suffering and is always on the side of the suffering man and woman, acted to give life back to Jesus. If human beings killed him, we need to remember that God has awakened him. This is the earliest, probably the very first, affirmation of the resurrection of Jesus as recorded in 1 Thessalonians 1:10, and it was always phrased as, "God has awakened him," or, "he has been awakened [raised]."[278] In conclusion, Schillebeeckx observes, "In early Christianity up to and including the New Testament, however, the emphasis was largely on God's saving act in raising Jesus from the dead. For the Christians *ho egeiras*—'God, who awakens to life'—became as it were a divine attribute, that is, a way of extolling God."[279]

In a nutshell, from Schillebeeckx one gathers the following: God does not want humanity to suffer. Being pure positivity, one cannot find any reason or motive for evil and suffering in God. Therefore, the cross is the index of the anti-divine in the world, and God opposes the crucifixion of Jesus as the epitome of evil. The ministry of healing, exorcism, open table fellowship, forgiveness, and compassion of his Son demonstrates God's goodness and radical opposition to evil and suffering. The violent death of Jesus is not

---

[277] Edward Schillebeeckx, The Collected Works of Edward Schillebeeckx Volume 6: Jesus: An Experiment in Christology, loc. 12782.

[278] Cf. Edward Schillebeeckx, The Collected Works of Edward Schillebeeckx Volume 6: Jesus: An Experiment in Christology, loc. 12779.

[279] Ibid, loc. 12782–12786.

God's doing but humanity's. No one should ascribe to God what has, in fact, been done to Jesus by the history of human injustice.[280] Finally, Jesus's resurrection is the final statement of God's goodness and his opposition to evil.

There are three fundamental things to recall. Tradition and experience have played a tremendous role in how God was understood and interpreted in the Old and in the New Testament and later tradition. Schillebeeckx in a brilliant way, looking at the reality of the world, established two principles to help unlock a missed or not much-known perspective of the divine truth. For him, contrast experiences and the world's movements toward a better way of life suggest the ultimate unmatchable goodness of God and God's rejection of evil. But to establish his theorem, Schillebeeckx postulates the eternal newness of God, a freshness expressed through his reinterpretation or narration of the life of Jesus. All this he hopes will help Jesus and his historical body, the Church, to regain credibility in the world.

---

[280] Cf. Edward Schillebeeckx, Christ, the Experience of Jesus as Lord, 728.

Chapter 5

The Cross in Marthe Robin the Stigmatic: Maybe God Is the Author of Human Suffering

The appearance of stigmata on some Christians is a mysterious event that has been difficult to explain. Luckily, it is not a common occurrence. A limited number of uniquely spiritual Christians have been fortunate, or unfortunate as the case may be, to bear those marks of the crucified Lord. The first documented case is that of St. Francis of Assisi in the thirteenth century. His stigmata appeared at a time when popular spirituality invited Christians to identify with the suffering of Christ as a way of demonstrating love of God and of neighbor. Marthe Robin (1902–1981), one of the last stigmatics, was also imprinted with the painful wounds of the suffering Christ. From the perspective of our reflection on the source and meaning of suffering, the ensuing question is, how much responsibility, if any, does God, or Jesus, have in the suffering of these stigmatics? Could Marthe Robin's declaration, "O Jesus, you have made me your little victim"[281] suggest to us an answer to this question?

5.1. Era of Mystical Experiences: Stigmata

Three hundred twenty-one (321) is the number of stigmatics recorded by the French doctor Imbert-Gourbeyer between the thirteenth century and the nineteenth century. The list begins from the thirteenth century because it is maintained that St. Francis of Assisi

---

[281] René Biot, The Enigma of the Stigmata, 1st ed. (NY: Hawthorn Books, 1962), 47.

was the first to have received the stigmata. History records that one day in 1224, as St. Francis was praying on the Mount of Alvernia, he had a vision. "Thereafter, [...he] bore on his hands and feet and side the marks of the wounds of the Crucifixion."[282] The stigmata of St. Francis should not come as a surprise to us, especially in the light of what was discussed to a large extent in the second chapter: St. Francis's spiritual attachment to the humanity of Jesus.

Prior to the St. Francis's experience, however, is the unsolved case of St. Paul. Some scholars believe Paul's statement, "I bear on my body the marks of Jesus," recorded in Galatians 6:17, literally means he was a stigmatic. Others, however, disagree with that. René Biot summarizes the discussion this way:

> Expert commentators agree in thinking that by these words [—I bear on my body the marks of Jesus—] he [Paul] means to denote the marks of the blows[283] he has received as painful guerdon of the witness he bore to his membership in Christ, and that the word he uses—in Greek, *stigmata*—had not the specialized sense it has since acquired. Some other interpreters see in this phrase a revelation of a "spiritual stigmata," that is, the suffering he bears in union with the Redeemer.[284]

---

[282] Ibid, 18.

[283] See 2 Corinthians 11:23–27, where Paul describes all the troubles he's been through as part of being an apostle of Christ. He says, "Are they servants of Christ? I am a better one—I am talking like a madman—with far greater labors, far more imprisonments, with countless beatings, and often near death. Five times I received at the hands of the Jews the forty lashes less one. Three times I was beaten with rods. Once I was stoned. Three times I was shipwrecked; a night and a day I was adrift at sea; on frequent journeys, in danger from rivers, danger from robbers, danger from my own people, danger from Gentiles, danger in the city, danger in the wilderness, danger at sea, danger from false brothers; in toil and hardship, through many a sleepless night, in hunger and thirst, often without food, in cold and exposure."

[284] René Biot, The Enigma of the Stigmata, 18.

Whether St. Paul was a stigmatic or not may never be known. But we all know that after the experience of St. Francis on Mount Alvernia, there was, in the words of Rene Biot, "a sort of explosion"[285] of cases of people bearing the painful marks of the crucified Lord. Thus, by the end of the thirteenth century, there were thirty-one other cases. The fourteenth century recorded a total of twenty-two cases, while the fifteenth century gives us an account of twenty-five cases. In the nineteenth century, more than twenty-nine cases were documented.[286] While the Church in her wisdom and prudence has neither beatified nor canonized a lot of those stigmatics, almost all of them claim their stigmata to be a sign of their identification with Jesus. We note that according to Doctor Imbert-Gourbeyer, only sixty-two of those 321 stigmatists have been canonized or beatified.[287] The twentieth century, however, gives the testimony of mystics like Theresa Neumann, Padre Pio, and Marthe Robin. "Since that time, numerous others—Padre Pio, Theresa Neumann, and Martha Robin, etc.—have borne the marks of Jesus crucified, either partially or completely, as invisible or external wounds upon their bodies."[288] Of them, only Padre Pio was canonized (June 16, 2002) and is consequently a saint. As for Theresa Neumann, the proceedings for her beatification commenced on February 13, 2005. Marthe Robin was recognized as "Venerable" on November 7, 2014.

As already mentioned in the second chapter, to identify with the human Christ, but most especially with the suffering Lord, was the dominant spirituality of the medieval era. Arnold I. Davidson and Maggie Fritz-Morkin rightly suggest,

> As many historians have maintained, the introduction of this new form of mysticism must be linked to a changed attitude and a new devotion towards the humanity of Christ, his Incarnation,

---

[285] Ibid.

[286] Cf. René Biot, The Enigma of the Stigmata, 18.

[287] Cf. Michael Freze, They Bore the Wounds of Christ: The Mystery of the Sacred Stigmata (Huntington, Ind.: Our Sunday Visitor, 1989), 11.

[288] Michael Freze, They Bore the Wounds of Christ, 11.

his Passion and, more generally, the corpo-
real existence that characterizes him as human.
However, we must avoid interpreting this new
kind of mystical experience as merely the consequence of a new theoretical elaboration regarding
Christ's humanity because it reflects a different
way of living and experiencing the humanity of
Christ; it is an experience that has theoretical
foundations but cannot be reduced to them. As
Pierre Hadot has argued, it is necessary to distin-
guish between the rational theological discourse
on the transcendent and the spiritual experience
of the transcendent. Mystical ecstasy must not
be confused with theological argumentation
and discourse; the methods and procedures of
philosophy and theology were traditionally in
the service of a new way of life that required a
transformation of one's very being. Regarding
the new forms of mysticism, we may appropriate the words of Giangiorgio Pasqualotto, spoken
in a quite different context: "it never concerns
only intellectual knowledge, but knowledge that
at every moment involves one's whole existence,
that is, which determines not only a new theory
but a new *experience*."[289]

While theories about the humanity and divinity of Christ were
good for the intellectuals of the Middle Ages, they did not appeal
much to the average Christian. For them, what they read and heard
about Jesus—how he was born in a manger, how he interacted with
people, how he carried his cross and died—was what fueled their
daily lives. This Jesus, whether human or divine, was what they knew.

---

[289] Davidson, Arnold I., and Maggie Fritz-Morkin. "Miracles of Bodily
Transformation, or How St. Francis Received the Stigmata," Critical Inquiry
35, no. 3 (January 2009), 452.

Stigmata and the pains and sufferings that come with them are not humanly or deliberately made. They are a spiritual but also a physical imprint of the marks of Christ's passion and crucifixion *received* by some few extremely devoted Christians. Ted Harrison, who wrote the story of Ethel Chapman, a stigmatic of the twentieth century, describes stigmata in the following words.

> The stigmata are wounds of Christ which have appeared on the hands, feet, on the side and around the head of a selected number of individuals during the course of Christian history. The marks correspond to the injuries inflicted on Christ during the passion by the nails, the spear and the crown of thorns. *The marks are not deliberately made and usually appear spontaneously at a time of great devotion, agony or ecstasy.* Not all stigmatists *receive* the marks in the same way.[290]

Ian Wilson maintains, "Stigmatics are professed to bear on their bodies replications of the crucified injuries suffered by Jesus."[291] Whether replications or real injuries, one common thing from the stigmatics is that the wounds bleed and are painful. René Biot suggests that pain is never absent.[292] And he continues, "Often, the pain becomes so severe that it forces the sufferer to cry out."[293] Marthe

---

[290] Ted Harrison, The Marks of the Cross: The Story of Ethel Chapman and the Stigmata (London: Darton, Longman and Todd, 1981), 1, with added emphasis. The appearance of this word "receive" implies the act of giving by someone and thus raises a lot of questions. Who gives? Is this a gift from the same God who did not put his Son on the cross? Is this a gift of the Son who knows that his Father did not put him on the cross? If indeed the Triune God does not want humanity to suffer, then why make these suffer?

[291] Ian Wilson, Stigmata: An Investigation into the Mysterious Appearance of Christ's Wounds in Hundreds of People from Medieval Italy to Modern America, 1st U.S. ed. (SF: Harper & Row, 1989), ix.

[292] Cf. Rene Biot, The Enigma of the Stigmata., 1st ed. (NY: Hawthorn Books, 1962), 53.

[293] Ibid, 54.

herself describes her stigmatization experience in similar words. She says, "The intensity of the suffering was such that it caused me to tremble dreadfully, all my limbs shook and I felt as if my heart were burning."[294] The wounds sustained also "give rise to flows of blood, varying in their abundance from one stigmatic to another. It must also be noted that, generally speaking, the quantity of blood thus emitted may be much more abundant than that which flows from an ordinary erosion of the teguments."[295] Multiple witnesses who saw Marthe after she was stigmatized, when interviewed in relation to her process of canonization, testified to have seen her bleeding. Father Peyrous Bernard, the postulator, reports,

> Some of those present were to leave sometimes quite detailed testimonies. Over fifty people questioned at the cause for beatification had seen blood flowing from Marthe's wounds. Mlle Faure, for example, a teacher at a private school in Saint-Uze said: "I saw blood flowing from her eyes." Canon Bérardier stated: "We saw her sweating blood from her forehead and tears of blood flowing sometimes thickly, leaving heavy traces across her cheeks, and sometimes mixed with ordinary tears." Abbé Auric wrote: "I personally witnessed her face all bloodstained: blood running from the stigmata of the crown of thorns, blood being wept from her eyes onto her cheeks." During the medical examination in 1942 the doctors also noted the presence of stigmata on her head, face and hands, and a large bloodstain on her chest.[296]

---

[294] Bernard Peyrous, Marthe Robin: A Prophetic Vision of the Gospel Message, trans. Kathryn Spink (Dublin: Veritas Publications, 2010), loc. 840.

[295] Rene Biot, The Enigma of the Stigmata, 55.

[296] Bernard Peyrous, Marthe Robin: A Prophetic Vision of the Gospel Message, loc. 845.

The stigmatics suffer greatly the pains that Jesus went through. Thus, the tension created between being one with Christ and the pain they suffer makes them both victims and privileged people. "[T]he philosopher and academician, Jean Guitton reports having questioned her [Marthe]: 'But,' I said to her, 'they say that the stigmata are simultaneously very joyful and very painful.'—'Yes, simultaneously. But you mustn't think of a human or sensory joy. It is a deep and 'divine' joy, a joy that is entirely internal. Similarly the suffering is extreme, primarily interior. If God did not support you, you would die.'"[297] It is perhaps in this regard that Fr. Jean-François Hüe, during an interview given about the life of Marthe Robin, stated, "Stigmatics are both victims and privileged people."[298] Are they victims of God's manifestations, the devil's machination, or simply victims of their desire to be privileged people by identifying with Jesus?

5.2. The Experience of Marthe Robin

Unlike Francis of Assisi, but like most of the stigmatics, Marthe Robin was and remained sick for most of her lifetime. According to Père Bernard Peyrous, the postulator of the beatification cause of Marthe, throughout her lifetime, "[s]he goes through series of psychological, familial, physical, as well as, spiritual suffering."[299]

5.2.1. The Birth and Family of Marthe

The Robins lived in Châteauneuf, in a region known as "The Plain," where religion, at that time, was hardly practiced. The Robins "were small landowners, having less than fourteen acres. They were simple people who did not occasion much comment and were a very

---

[297] Ibid, loc. 840.

[298] Jean-François Hüe, La Foi Pris au Mot: Marthe Robin, accessed July 8, 2016, https://www.youtube.com/watch?v=IBprV7tQXCw&t=1423s.

[299] Père Bernard Peyrous, "Marthe Robin: Une Vie si Fragile si Feconde," https://www.youtube.com/watch?v=ff1IX7LZG2o) Accessed March 8, 2018. The translation is mine. The original is "Elle traverse toute une série de souffrance physiologique, familiale, physique, spirituel aussi."

social family. Joseph, the father, was 'a large man, jovial and unaffected,' a tiny bit dictatorial [...] 'He was devout and reactionary.' 'No, he was anticlerical!' others will tell you."[300] Mrs. Robin, whose maiden name was Amélie-Célectine Chosson, "'was a small woman with a round head like a bird's, that was always covered with a bonnet.' 'Reserved and placid, she seldom went out.' But she loved to laugh."[301]

Marthe Louise Robin was born in Châteauneuf-de-Galaure on March 13, 1902, the last born of a family of six children. The eldest child of the family was Célina, followed by Gabrielle. Alice was the third child, who according to Raymond Peyret was "the closest to Marthe."[302] The fourth child and the only boy of the family was Henry. Clémence was the fifth child of the family. The parents of Marthe "were simple, humble peasants who saw to it that their family received a solid Christian foundation."[303] "According to some accounts [which cannot be verified] the advent of the little Marthe into the world, far from being a cause for celebration, provoked an argument between Mr. and Mrs. Robin. One can easily appreciate that this sixth birth in a family of poor farmers must have seemed a heavy burden."[304]

5.2.2. The Early Crosses of Marthe

Three weeks after her birth, Marthe was baptized on Holy Saturday of April 5, 1902. Besides the fact that her birth, even if for just a short while, was a sign of division in her family, in 1903 the gates of hell broke loose. A typhoid epidemic broke in the village. It killed Clémence, one of Marthe's sisters, and made Alice very sick. It is said, "Marthe was not spared either, and although she recovered she

---

[300] Raymond Peyret, Marthe Robin: The Cross and the Joy (NY: Alba House, 1983), 10.

[301] Ibid, 12.

[302] Ibid.

[303] Michael Freze, They Bore the Wounds of Christ: The Mystery of the Sacred Stigmata, 284.

[304] Raymond Peyret, Marthe Robin: The Cross and the Joy, 15

remained frail thereafter."[305] History holds that Marthe never completed her elementary education because she was sick during the final exam. Reverend Raymond Peyret writes, "Marthe was frequently ill so that she missed classes two or three days [a week] in succession. She also had to help her mother who often suffered from billow attacks [...] Marthe never received her diploma [...] she was sick on the day of final examination."[306] When the time came for Marthe to receive her first Holy Communion, which would have been in 1911, she missed it because she was again sick. Michael Freze suggests that Marthe's First Communion was postponed because she was sick with measles.[307] She finally received Jesus in Communion a year later, on August 15, 1912. Prior to that, however, on May 3, 1911, Bishop Chesnelong of Valence had conferred on Marthe the gifts of the Holy Spirit through the sacrament of Confirmation that he administered in her parish that year. Her Solemn Communion, now known in France even today as *Profession de foi*, was held in 1914.

5.2.3. Marthe's Disposition to Live a Happy Life

Despite the multiple setbacks due to the bad health of Marthe, she seemed to have been determined to make the best out of it. She was not resigned to what she was going through, rather just like all the little girls of her time, she played at digging holes in the ground, at hopscotch, at jumping the rope, and even at waving at unknown people in the train passing through her village.

> Marthe was a great one for playing. All her schoolmates said that she was happy and full of life. And she was rather mischievous, too. One day, at Châteauneuf fair, she entertains herself by pinning a rabbit tail on a man's back. She had wanted to attach a piece of paper with something

---

[305] Ibid, 16.

[306] Ibid, 18.

[307] Cf. Michael Freze, They Bore the Wounds of Christ: The Mystery of the Sacred Stigmata, 285.

written on it, but couldn't find a pencil to write. So she used the rabbit tail instead.[308]

Marthe did not only enjoy playing with the age mates, she also enjoyed doing what the family did for a living. She enjoyed helping her parents, not just at home but also in the fields. After leaving school, "Marthe enjoyed her work as a Shepherdess."[309] This was an activity that, later on when she confided to Marie-Ange Dumas, she claimed gave her a lot of time to engage in mental prayer. Well, for one coming from a religious family, what does she do with idle time? She certainly prays. But there is no suggestion that Marthe spent her childhood or adolescence simply praying or contemplating. In fact, we are invited to appreciate that, like her friends, Marthe danced at all the home parties that were held in her neighborhood during winter.[310]

> During her adolescence, Marthe was extremely fun-loving. Max Achard, who was the son of her neighbor, and almost her own age, recalls: "All Robin girls were playful; they loved to laugh. Their paternal grandmother was like that also; she loved to see children enjoying themselves, and she enthralled them by humming tunes with nonsense words making time with her hands for singing and dancing. Joseph Robin himself was a happy person who loved company."[311]

Marthe's fun-loving and playful nature, despite her sickly physique, may later serve to help us understand her entire "suffering" life. It is unlikely that one who enjoyed company with age mates, fun, laughter, and the outside world, would desire to embrace pain, suffering, and confinement to a bed in an almost-dark room.

---

[308] Raymond Peyret, Marthe Robin: The Cross and the Joy, 19.

[309] Ibid, 21.

[310] Ibid, 22.

[311] Ibid, 21.

5.2.4. The Cross of Marthe

In May 1918, when she was sixteen years old, Marthe began to have her first headaches.[312] On November 25 of the same year,

> [w]hen Marthe was with her mother in the kitchen, she fell and was unable to get up unassisted [...] What strange malady had attacked Marthe? Throughout the whole day she did not eat or speak; her legs were paralyzed, and she was unconscious. Was it an attack of polio, meningitis, or rheumatoid arthritis? "She suffered so, the poor soul," recalls her niece, Mrs. Danthony of Anneyron. "We heard her cry out!" Sometimes she cried out; more often she slept; perhaps it was encephalitis. This state of affairs lasted for seventeen months, according to some; for twenty-seven months according to others.[313]

Whether Marthe was sick for seventeen or twenty-seven months, she was undoubtedly in good-enough shape by spring 1922 to have visited her sister Gabrielle for eight good days. It was during her time at the sisters' place that

> [o]ne day she climbed up into the hayloft and rummaged through a trunk that was there, finding therein an old spiritual book. Her eyes fell upon a sentence, the gist of which was *"You look for joy, peace, and sweetness; but it is suffering for which you must prepare."* (This was apparently the *Imitation of Christ*. The sentence reported orally by two of Marthe's friends is much like *Imitation*, Book II, Chapter X, Verse I: "Dispose thy self to

---

[312] Cf. Raymond Peyret, Marthe Robin: The Cross and the Joy, 25.
[313] Ibid, 25–26.

patience, rather than consolation; and to carrying the cross, rather than goodness.") It came to
her like a flash of lightning. "For you," Marthe
said to herself, "it will be suffering."[314]

Even when Marthe felt better physically, spiritually, and psy-
chologically, she was reminded that her lot was pain and suffering.
Commenting on Marthe's encounter with the phrase, "You look for
joy, peace, and sweetness; but it is suffering for which you must pre-
pare," Jean Barbier asks a fundamental question.

> Marthe va-t-elle devoir quitter sa vie familiale, sa
> vie d'écolier, sa vie de ménagère et d'entraide...,
> donc la joie pour affronter l'austérité de la souf-
> france [?] Toujours est-il que cette petite phrase
> issue d'un vieux parchemin la fait réfléchir, c'est
> dans le tréfonds de la pensée et du coeur que se
> forgent les idées. La phrase est breve, coupante
> [...] Va-t-il falloir ôter toutes les branches fleuries
> mais inutiles, pour entrevoir l'arbre d'hiver lourd
> de sacrifices[?][315]

For Barbier, "[w]as Marthe now to leave family life, school life,
life of a housekeeper, and helper,...so much joy to face austerity
and suffering?" Such a question for a young little girl who braved
all the troubles of her health to enjoy a happy life was legitimate.
Marthe wasn't ready to let go of her dreams of a normal happy life.

---

[314] Ibid, 29, with added emphasis.

[315] Jean Barbier, Trois Stigmatisés: Thérèse Neumann, Le Padre Pio, Marthe Robin
(Paris: Téqui, 1987), 94. The translation which is mine is, "Will Marthe have to
leave her family life, her school life, her life as a housekeeper and a helper..., so
the joy to face the austerity of suffering [?] Still, this little sentence from an old
manual makes her reflect, it is in the depths of thought and heart that ideas are
forged. The sentence is brief, cutting [...] Will it be that she needs to remove all
the branches flowered but useless, to make way for the heavy winter sacrificial
tree[?]"

So despite all the troubles, Marthe lived in the hope of being well. But her strange and mysterious illness also acted bizarrely. It sometimes receded, giving the impression of going away, and then suddenly came back. Very soon, Marthe had to face the reality of a severe relapse with the multiple recurrences and aggravation of her sickness.

In the autumn of the same year, precisely, "[o]n October 30, 1922, intense pain began once more in Marthe's knees and the paralysis again set in."[316] When she was twenty-three years old (in August 1925), she was given an opportunity to go on a pilgrimage in Lourdes. But at the last moment, having learned that another sick person in Châteauneuf wanted badly a chance to go to the pilgrimage in Lourdes, Marthe sacrificed her place.[317] For Raymond Peyret,

> [t]his renunciation, which signified such a great love, marks quietly but surely the spiritual turning point of Marthe Robin. The interior struggle, begun at Saint-Péray, against the demands of God, ended up with her unconditional surrender. From then on, everything was in readiness for the hour of her consecration.[318]

On October 15, 1925, the feast day of St. Teresa of Avila and the year of the canonization of the French Saint Thérèse of Lisieux by Pope Pius XI, Marthe made a move that was very strange. As if her pains and suffering were not enough, or maybe hoping for a healthier life, in her own words, "I dared, I chose Christ Jesus,"[319] she said. The original French would have sounded, "*J'ai osé, j'ai osé choisir Jesus.*" Was this choice another devotion of identification with the humanity of Christ? For "an uneducated" French lady of the early twentieth century, this was most likely neither a valid nor relevant question. Even though later on, "[o]n 4 April 1932 she wrote: 'I am

---

[316] Raymond Peyret, Marthe Robin: The Cross and the Joy, 31.

[317] Cf. Raymond Peyret, Marthe Robin: The Cross and the Joy, 36.

[318] Ibid, 36.

[319] Véronica Beaulieu, Marthe Robin, accessed July 8, 2016, https://www.youtube.com/watch?v=NQlOj5BpaXs.

sure of the human presence of Jesus at my side.'"[320] For her, Jesus was Jesus, nothing less, nothing more. Whatever the case was, her choice of Jesus was sealed through the *Act of Abandonment to the Love and the Will of God.*"[321] Through the act, she declared her readiness to offer everything to God and receive everything from him.[322] "She gave to the Lord her memory, her intelligence, her will, her heart, her body, and all her faculties."[323] And she was ready to receive whatever the Lord would give: "pain, sorrow, joy, consolation, dryness, shame, desertion, scorn, humiliation, work, suffering, trials, everything that comes to me from you, everything that you wish, O Jesus."[324]

At this stage, one would think that the God who healed the sick, as his method of showing his disgust against evil, would miraculously make her well again, give joy or grant consolation, and hide in his bosom a servant who abandons herself into his hand. That didn't seem to be the case of Marthe Robin.

"Barely a year after having made the act of abandonment to the will of God, Marthe again fell gravely ill."[325] On October 3, 1926, a doctor was called to examine Marthe's condition. He is quoted to have said, "There is nothing more that can be done,"[326] for her. Three weeks later, she pulled out of the coma into which she was plunged on October 3. But this time, she was almost unable to do anything on her own. While she still maintained some form of mobility in her legs and arms, it was impossible, she says, to make the least movement without the help of her devoted mama.[327] She was always in pain. And since misfortune never comes alone, on March 25, 1928, her legs contracted and twisted out of shape, becoming fully paralyzed.

---

[320] Bernard Peyrous, Marthe Robin: A Prophetic Vision of the Gospel Message, loc. 903.
[321] There are two versions of this act. One may read in appendix 1 the first version which is most likely the one Marthe prayed at this point.
[322] Cf. Raymond Peyret, Marthe Robin: The Cross and the Joy, 38.
[323] Ibid, 38.
[324] Ibid, 39.
[325] Ibid, 41.
[326] Ibid.
[327] Cf. Raymond Peyret, Marthe Robin: The Cross and the Joy, 42.

As though this paralysis was not sufficient Calvary for her, Marthe ceased eating altogether [...] From 1928 to 1981, the year of her death, Marthe did not consume anything except the Eucharist that was brought to her once or twice a week. The host, entering into her, instantly disappeared without any normal ingestion. Marthe could not swallow anything else.[328]

---

[328] Ibid, 44. There are medical reports about the phenomenon of Marthe not eating anything at the exception of Communion. But Raymond Peyret indicates in his book that the report prepared by Dr. Bansillon, Dr. Richard, and Dr. Dechaume, three highly qualified professors, has not yet been released to the public. See Raymond Peyret, Marthe Robin: The Cross and the Joy, 56. Bernard Peyrous explains, "Once her illness had fully progressed, no one ever saw Marthe eat. She might perhaps have availed herself of the fruit in her room but no evidence has been found to that effect. Nor is there anything to suggest that she drank. Nothing to indicate she did so has been discovered. Of course this gave rise to questions. For some it had to be a hoax. But the vast majority of people who came to Châteauneuf believed that she did not eat or drink. There were those who would have liked a public demonstration of this fact in order to convince unbelievers that the miraculous was possible. The Parisian neuropsychiatrist, Doctor Assailly, who was very fond of Marthe, came to see her in 1949 and later wrote a report of their discussion: "'Mademoiselle,' I said to her in a tone for which I would subsequently reproach myself, "not for the world do I doubt your honesty but you must understand that as a doctor I would love to be able to put you in a clinic for a month or two, to convince my colleagues of the reality of the extraordinary phenomena you are presenting. This sort of witness could also be part of your mission, and your testimony would carry some weight with non-believers and with the majority of Catholics who put such manifestations down to deception... Conscious or otherwise," he added condescendingly. Marthe remained silent so Doctor Assailly renewed his request, specifying that ideally she would be observed by both Catholic and nonbelieving doctors. Still Marthe said nothing. Then she said softly, "Doctor, I have only one rule: that of obedience. If my spiritual director, my bishop or obviously the Holy Father, were to decide that I should be hospitalized, I would say yes at once and you could take me wherever you wished. But do you really think that the problem lies where you are looking for it?" Then in response to another remark by the doctor, she said: "No, Doctor, that's not where the problem is."'" See Bernard Peyrous, Marthe Robin: A Prophetic Vision of the Gospel Message, loc. 4238–4252.

Bernard Peyrous explains, "When people tried to make her drink, she said, 'I feel such a violent pain that it makes me cry out despite myself'. She suffered constantly. On 5 December 1930 she wrote: 'I am having very violent pain all over, principally in my head, stomach and back.'"[329] The pain, the inability to eat, and the paralysis of her feet were not the end of Marthe's troubles. For on February 2, 1929, Marthe ended up losing the mobility of her hands. In summary:

> Her arms and legs held her down in her bed; her legs were partly bent; she was twisted, with a pillow under her back, and a stiff cushion to support her knees; her right arm lay across her chest, and her left arm was stretched out along her body. She could not move [...] Marthe endured torments and pain as soon as she was lifted [whenever the beddings were to be changed...] In this uncomfortable and unchangeable position, Marthe remained without drinking, without eating, and without sleeping, for more than fifty years.[330]

Of all the suffering that Marthe had to go through, the most tragic of them all was the loss of the use of her hands. When this happened, she said, "I desperately wanted to die."[331] For the last drop of dignity that Marthe preserved through her activity of needling had become impossible. She had to resign to complete dependence, which—according to Bernard Peyrous—made her feel she had lost her dignity. He writes,

---

[329] Bernard Peyrous, Marthe Robin: A Prophetic Vision of the Gospel Message, loc. 730.

[330] Raymond Peyret, Marthe Robin: The Cross and the Joy, 46–47.

[331] Bernard Peyrous, Marthe Robin: A Prophetic Vision of the Gospel Message, loc. 734.

She did not resign herself easily to total dependence: "Must I then give up my dear needlework forever? I did so love it. It preserved a small illusion of activity. It was another reason to live; and it was needlework that taught me the totally divine art of contemplation…and the no less divine art of being ever joyful. My poor little nature, which has always remained so active and so courageous in affliction, hardly dares to face the prospect of an irrevocable inability to work." These thoughts are manifestly very human, in the positive sense. Marthe Robin was not a glorious body. She did not live like the angels. She needed a minimum amount of activity and occupation and her dignity was important to her. It was extremely hard for her to be regarded as a complete cripple.[332]

In the face of such torment and pain, Marthe did not believe that she was a victim of the devil's wicked machinery in the world. Rather, she maintains that Jesus has made her his victim.

"Oh Jesus, you have made me your little victim," she said on July 12, 1929, "as you have wished to be mine and that of all mankind. All my life, O my God is yours…O Cross, Cross of my savior…O divine ladder that joins earth to heaven, you are the altar upon which I must consume my sacrifice and consume my life in immolation and love."[333]

And maybe to unmistakably prove that God had indeed made Marthe his victim, "at the end of September 1930, Jesus appeared to

---

[332] Ibid, loc. 730–734.
[333] Raymond Peyret, Marthe Robin: The Cross and the Joy, 47.

Marthe and asked her, 'Do you wish to become like me?'"[334] We can only guess her answer from her previous act of abandonment and the subsequent occurrences which are here recounted:

> Sometime during the early part of October (possibly on the feast day of Saint Francis, the stigmatized saint), Jesus crucified appeared before the eyes of Marthe. At once he took her paralyzed arms, rigid since February 2, 1929, and opened them wide. At that moment a tongue of flame leaped from his side, separated in two, and struck both her feet and both her hands; the third tongue of flame stuck Marthe on the heart. She bled from her hands, her feet, and her heart. Later—whether it was the same day is not known—Jesus imported his crown of thorns on Marthe's head. The marks extended down to her eyes and bled freely [...] Still later, Jesus intervened again, imposing upon Marthe the wood of the Cross; Marthe felt crushed—dislocated.[335]

We should keep in mind that according to Marthe's experience and account of events, Jesus—the glorified Lord, both divine and glorified human—is the one who imprints on her the marks of his crucifixion. Why would Jesus do such a thing to someone who consecrated herself to him? Why would a God who hates suffering and stands on our side, humanity's side, against pain and evil put his servant through such unbearable suffering? René Biot notes that pain "is never absent whatever the form of stigmatization. It is always intense."[336] Examining the medical records, and the account of Marthe's paralysis and stigmata, for her canonization, a hospice specialist noted, "This woman [Marthe] suffered as much as a human

---

[334] Ibid, 51.
[335] Ibid, 52.
[336] René Biot, The Enigma of the Stigmata, 53.

being could suffer."[337] There is absolutely no doubt about that. Marthe's conversations with her beloved spiritual director Fr. Finet[338] attest to these intense times of pain and suffering. The discussions took place most of the time on Thursdays as Marthe was about to enter into agony. "Fr. Finet more than once told of his pathetic dialogue between them that preceded her entry into the pain of the passion: 'Father, do you know that today is Thursday?' 'Yes, my child.' 'You know, Father, that this evening…' 'Yes, my child.' 'Father, I will not be able to bear it.' 'Yes, my child!'"[339] A witness's description of Marthe's suffering and pain comes from another priest:

> Canon Bérardier, director of charitable works for the diocese and then priest in charge of the parish of Saint-Louis in the city of Saint-Etienne. In 1942 he wrote: "Friday at 4.15 p.m. official time, i.e., 2.15 p.m. by the sun. We joined M. Finet who had been with Marthe for over two hours… A continuous moan was coming from Marthe's lips; a lament that could be perfectly noted in a musical score, with crescendos and diminuendos. This repeated sound quickly seized hold of and haunted the heart. Doctor Ricard told us that this kind of moaning is an indication of pain exacerbated in the extreme. This is how a person moans when he can no longer cry out, an expression of suffering beyond relief. At the same time Marthe's head moved slowly and regularly from

---

337 Père Bernard Peyrous, "Marthe Robin: Une Vie si Fragile si Feconde," https://www.youtube.com/watch?v=ff1IX7LZG2o).

338 Fr. Georges Finet, a priest from Lyon. He became the spiritual director of Marthe Robin in 1936. And he remained her spiritual director until she died in 1981.

339 Raymond Peyret, Marthe Robin: The Cross and the Joy, 55.

right to left on her pillow, and at times her body would jerk in all directions."[340]

Marthe was suffering physically, but she was also always emotionally terrified and overwhelmed by the pains that she was to go through during these days of agony.

5.2.5. Instances of the Presence of the Devil in Marthe's Life

What is most difficult to understand and interpret about Marthe's suffering is the mention of the devil in several instances. Satan is alluded to in specific and distinct occurrences in the life of Marthe. Sometime between November 2, 1928, and February 2, 1929, the devil appeared to Marthe for the first time and, striking her a blow with his fist, broke two of her teeth.[341] "Père Faure wrote: 'The devil, after reproaching her in the usual way, slapped her face, even breaking two of her teeth, and cursed her.'"[342] The only direct physical pain, it seems, inflicted to Marthe by the devil is the breaking of her two teeth. The appearance of Satan only at this stage of Marthe's life makes her entire story not merely more complicated and mysterious, but it also validates her victimization. For if Satan is part of the picture only now, then who or what has been the cause of the sickly and weak health condition of Marthe? God?

Bernard Peyrous reports another instance of the devil's interaction with Marthe. He states,

> [O]n 27 February 1930 she [Marthe] wrote: "The devil sniggers lugubriously into my ears, repeating foul words without interruption or rest: he tells me I should not believe there is a place for

---

[340] Bernard Peyrous, Marthe Robin: A Prophetic Vision of the Gospel Message, loc. 876–881.

[341] Raymond Peyret, Marthe Robin: The Cross and the Joy, 46.

[342] Bernard Peyrous, Marthe Robin: A Prophetic Vision of the Gospel Message, loc. 716.

me in Paradise. He also tells me that I should not imagine that God loves me. He attacks me too by way of thirst, making me cruelly and excessively thirsty, which is a very painful battle for me."[343]

It is important to note that at this time Marthe was already unable to eat and drink. Was she attributing to the devil the lack of what physiologically a body needs for survival? Every single human being needs water and food to survive. And when one does neither drink nor eat, it is understandable that one feels hungry and thirsty. But considering the fact that Marthe lived fifty to fifty-one years—on Communion only—without eating nor drinking, I wonder if the claim of the devil making her extremely thirsty wasn't blaming him for something natural?

The third instance of the direct manifestation of Satan is during her agony after she was marked with the signs of the crucified Lord. Raymond Peyret writes, "And little by little, during the course of that day on Thursday, Marthe increasingly felt the pangs of the Passion. She was in combat against the infernal regions unleashed, against the devil, who beat her head against the furniture near her couch."[344] Father Canon Bérardier, a witness in Bernard Peyrout's book, has a more violent description of the event. According to him, on Fridays during the agony, one

> heard Marthe say very distinctly: "Oh! Go away! Be quiet!" She was addressing the devil and her castigations were not unfounded because a few moments later, the previous painful lament gave way to a sort of raucous, almost savage cry which lasted several seconds. The lament was resumed, interrupted again by a "Be quiet" uttered in the same threatening tone. Sometimes Marthe would add: "Oh you! Will you keep quiet! You won't get

---

[343] Ibid, loc. 712–716.
[344] Raymond Peyret, Marthe Robin: The Cross and the Joy, 55.

anywhere!" No doubt at that point Satan was suggesting the temptation of despair to her and trying to persuade her that her suffering was in vain.[345]

These attacks of the devil during the agony are hard to interpret. How can God make Marthe suffer the pains of the crucifixion and still not defend her from Satan? It seems that the devil fights Marthe because she suffers. Isn't that strange from what we commonly know about the devil? Satan is meant to be happy when someone is suffering. And here he is, unhappy because Marthe is going through pain. Marthe's pain and torment are exponentially multiplied by the physical attacks of the devil who is at her heels because of the suffering inflicted on her by Christ.

5.3. Marthe's Interpretation of Her Suffering

It is essential to start this section by emphasizing that Marthe was very private. She did not see her suffering as a way of attracting attention. In fact, there are many instances that suggest Marthe tried in her little ways to hide it. Around September 1930, when she received the stigmata and started to bleed, Marthe would not allow her mother to mention or to say anything to anyone. She went as far as asking her mother not to mention it to the pastor of the parish known in French as "M. le Curé."

> During the 1930s Marthe's friend, Gisèle Signé, visited her at La Plaine: "One day, after parting from Marthe and saying goodbye, I left. I was in the courtyard. Mme Robin called out to me, 'Little one' and I turned round. 'I'd like to tell you something. I'm very worried about my little one. She's bleeding.' She indicated the heart, the face (forehead and eyes). I immediately thought,

---

[345] Bernard Peyrous, Marthe Robin: A Prophetic Vision of the Gospel Message, loc. 881–885.

'Those are the stigmata.'—'But what are the stigmata?' She thought it was an illness. 'Look at this linen,' she said to me. It was all blood-stained. 'I've washed this laundry,' Marthe's mother said. 'I've boiled it, I've bleached it but it won't come out. What is it?' – 'Mother Robin you should not keep this to yourself. Marthe should talk to M. le Curé about it.' She replied: 'Marthe doesn't want me to tell him, don't say anything about it to him.'"[346]

Writing to Sister Marie-Thérèse in the same year (1930), she begs the latter to pray for her. "I beg you, my sister Marie-Thérèse, to pray that no one will see how I suffer, neither my family nor those around me; I ask daily for this grace from the Blessed Virgin, and that she will continue to grant this: I implore you to ask this along with me."[347] From the proceedings, it is quite evident that Marthe's situation was not something she was faking to get people's attention. The stigmata, the suffering, and the pain that she went through had, for her, a much more profound meaning and significance.

Besides seeing herself in her sickness as a victim of God, Marthe understood her suffering as (1) a *school of the love* of God and the neighbor, (2) as a *reminder to people that being members of the body of Christ, we are called to share in his suffering as well.*

In 1927, Marthe explained that she seemed to be no more than a very tiny thing in the arms of God and that she will remain so until she dies.[348] In her notebook, which was only discovered after she died, she explained how her suffering has instructed her about Love. She wrote,

> My soul is plunged into and, as it were, swept away towards that Jerusalem of Love, by the

---

[346] Ibid, loc. 822–826.
[347] Raymond Peyret, Marthe Robin: The Cross and the Joy, 51.
[348] Cf. Raymond Peyret, Marthe Robin: The Cross and the Joy, 42.

powerful allurements and inspirations of God Himself, who now and then seems to desire to absorb me wholly into himself. I am afraid of all this!... I am so alone, spiritually and mentally, and meanwhile I understand that I must abandon myself to Him without any reservation. So be it! I have much need of this "Fiat." [Some few day later, she continues.] I taste how sweet it is to love, even in suffering, and I shall say a*bove all* in suffering; for suffering is an unsurpassed school of true love... It is the living language of Love, and the great teacher of humankind. One learns to love, and one does not really love except *in* and *by* suffering, for true suffering instructs us, not through human delights, but through the stripping away and renouncing of self on the Cross. A heart upon which pain has not imprinted its bleeding wounds cannot freely breathe the life-giving and sanctifying air of the summits and of Heaven. All ascents feed upon suffering that has been passed. To ascend is to pass beyond without ceasing... It is to give all and sacrifice all for God through Love.[349]

Some few years later, on the night of December 31, 1930, she says, "My whole being has undergone a transformation as mysterious as it is profound. A year of trials, a year of pain. A year of grace and of love. My real joy on my sickbed is profound, lasting because it is divine... I reflect upon the road I have traveled since the beginning of my illness, and from this reflection emerges only Love, gratitude toward God who is so merciful and so good. What a labor! What broth has God wrought in me! But what leaping of the heart, what death-struggles of the will it takes to die to self."[350] The Marthe who

---

[349] Ibid, 42–43.
[350] Ibid, 54.

wanted to die now implores for prayers. "Pray for me [she writes to Sister Marie Thérèse] so that I may learn to suffer for the salvation of souls, to suffer that Jesus may be loved."[351]

The second interpretation that Marthe gives to her suffering seems to have come last. It indeed came to her at a time where her situation was known to a lot of people who even came to visit her. Bernard Peyrous suggests that this interpretation of her painful stigmata was around the time of the Second World War (1939–1945). When people suffered because of the atrocities of the war, Marthe depicted herself as one reminding to the suffering masses of our Christian duty of sharing in the passion of Christ.

> Marthe herself gave an interpretation of her Passion in a conversation with Père Livragne, an Oratorian Father and a great preacher of retreats: "All Christians are called upon to participate in the Passion, to complete in their body that which is missing in the Passion of the whole Christ. I am just a sign, a reminder to Christians."[352]

We know that Marthe did a lot of reading either herself or through someone reading to her. "Marthe Robin read or had read to her, a number of books from the parish library."[353] Most of the books she read were spiritual books, some of which most likely those from Mlle Blanck might have been medieval spiritualities, of identification with the suffering Christ.

> So Marthe threw herself into what she had: books on spirituality, which were in any case better suited to her than theological works and fundamentally more in line with what she was seeking. The parish library bought up all the latest

---

[351] Ibid.

[352] Bernard Peyrous, Marthe Robin: A Prophetic Vision of the Gospel Message, loc. 871–876.

[353] Ibid, loc. 948.

publications and was well stocked with spiritual books. One of Marthe's friends, Mlle Blanck, who was very interested in mystics, also kept her supplied with books and pamphlets on the spirituality of the Sacred Heart and introduced her to the saintly Italian Sister, Bénigne Consolata of Como. Thus we know of some twenty books at least that Marthe went through. Sometimes they were the work of fashionable authors of the day such as the Jesuit Père Plus, Abbé Klein, Père Désiré des Planches and the Dominican Père Bernadot. They dealt with essential elements of the interior life, with the Eucharist and faith, but they were mostly concerned with different people's lives, their notes and correspondence. Some were very well-known: Saint Mechtilde von Hackeborn, Saint Teresa of Avila, Saint John of the Cross, Saint Marguerite-Marie, Catherine Emmerich, Saint Veronica Giuliani and Saint LouisMarie Grignion de Montfort. Others were only just making their appearance in the field of spirituality at that time: Madeleine Semer, Marie-Antoinette de Geuser, Gemma Galgani, Consummata, Adèle Garnier, Thérèse Durnerin, Lucie-Christine, Dina Belanger, Theresa Higginson, Elisabeth of the Trinity, and Thérèse of the Child Jesus, "her big sister" whom Marthe took great delight in reading. But she also had a deep grasp of the contents of the other works made available to her.[354]

All these books which she read after she had received the stigmata, it seems, helped her put words to what she was going through.

---

[354] Ibid, loc. 948–962.

Marthe did not just smoothly understand her situation. Initially she went through a lot of confusing, fearful, and disorientating moments. She wrote and expressed a lot of things that she did not understand, except that she was experiencing it. In 1930, Marthe explains how two years before she wanted to die so as to be relieved of her suffering and pain.

> "Two years ago," she said on 28 March 1930, "I desperately wanted to die in order to see God, because I had a firm hope of a blessed eternity. Now that I feel I have a mission to fulfill, I am fighting illness every inch of the way, offering up in advance the suffering that my energy and resignation are prolonging." On the human level, which for Marthe meant that of illness, the years 1929 and 1930 were thus a tragic time for her. She was all too well aware of it. "Two years of total incapacity are just up. What a cruel experience of renunciation it has been," she was to say on 2 February 1931. She did not escape into the spiritual at all. She did not create a parallel universe. Thanks to God's palpable intervention, however, they were also years of a great turning point in her life. Now, it should be emphasized, her spiritual life would no longer develop alongside her illness but actually within it. It was from her illness that she was to draw the meaning of her life. She had turned a dreadful situation right round and given it value. From then on she would be able not just to survive but actually to advance with all her energy. In her journal she wrote: "The physical and psychological suffering works, I believe, very effectively and very favorably on my spiritual activity and, since this new transformation, I think more about souls and unite myself better to them in God, praying

more than I did before for all of them but especially for sacerdotal souls, for priests, missionaries, religious, my special vocation, my beautiful mission of love."[355]

Apparently, the great turning point of Marthe's progressive spiritualization of her situation came sometime in 1928 when she received the visit of two Capuchin fathers. Fr. Bernard Peyrous reports,

En 1928…a la suite de la visite de deux pères capucins chez elle, elle reçois ce que nous appellerions une effusion de l'Esprit, qui comme St. Paul s'empare d'elle et elle accept. Tout d'un coup sa vie change complement. Elle comprend que sa vie peut être féconde si elle est uni a Jesus Christ et en particulier a la passion du Christ. A partir ce moment la, les paramètres change complètement, elle accept sa vie et la choisi… C'est une veritable revolution mental, une véritable revolution spirituelle qu'elle fais a ce moment la. Et elle comprend qu'au coeur de sa souffrance qu'elle sera féconde.[356]

What did the Capuchin fathers tell her? We may never know, but we know for a fact that from that moment on, Marthe stopped complaining about her illness. And she realized that through her sickness she was called to love. It is therefore not surprising to hear

---

[355] Ibid, loc. 734–744.

[356] Bernard Peyrous, "Marthe Robin: Une Vie si Fragile si Feconde." And the translation which is mine is, "In 1928…following the visit of two Capuchin fathers to her home, she receives what we would call an outpouring of the Spirit, which like in St. Paul's case seizes her and she accepts. All of a sudden, her life changes. She understands that her life can be fruitful if she is united with Jesus Christ and especially with the passion of Christ. From that moment on, the parameters changed completely, she accepts her life and chooses it… It is a real mental revolution, a real spiritual revolution that she is doing at this moment. And she understands that the heart of her suffering she will be fruitful."

her say, "I am covered with blood, [...] but I ardently accept the prolongation of my pilgrimage ... Oh! I would not wish to exchange my martyrdom for all the joys of the world and all the riches of the earth. I have only one desire: to save souls by loving God more and more."[357] For Marthe, her suffering was meant to lead her to love God. But she saw her pain as an opportunity to love neighbor by serving as a reminder to our call to share in Christ suffering for the salvation of others. Jean Barbier writes, "Elle partageait ansi la Passion du Christ. Elle s'identifiais à lui; devenait un autre Christ. Elle était comme crucifiée par la soufrance et par l'amour; car plus on aime, plus on souffre. Et quand on aime, il semble que les puissances de l'Enfer vous tombent dessus."[358]

As mysterious as the life of all stigmatics can be, Marthe Robin's is especially difficult to interpret. Who or what was responsible for Marthe's childhood sickness? Sin? But she was baptized three weeks after her birth and would have been incapable of sin when things, by 1903, started getting sour in her life. Human finitude? Then why don't all human beings go through the same troubles? God? How will we be able to make a case for that in the light of her contemporary Schillebeeckx, who maintained unequivocally that God is pure positivity and that there cannot be any proof, any reason for pain and suffering in God? In Marthe, there is no doubt, Jesus, the crucified and risen Lord, the Son of God and God, inflicted her with all the pains and sufferings of the Cross. The real question we are left with is, if God hates pain and suffering as we want to claim—with Schillebeeckx—or what good reason does he then inflict, if he actually does, on some people, in this case the stigmatics, with pain and suffering? If God never willed the suffering of his Son, as Schillebeeckx explains, for what reason does he inflict pain and suffering on the stigmatics? These are some few questions that the stigmatic's Marthe Robin's life raises vis-à-vis Schillebeeckx theology.

---

[357] Raymond Peyret, Marthe Robin: The Cross and the Joy, 50.

[358] Jean Barbier, Trois Stigmatisés, 100–101. The translation is mine: "She shared in the Passion of Christ. She identified with him, became another Christ. She was crucified by suffering and love because the more one loves, the more s/he suffers. And when one loves, it seems s/he is assailed by the powers of hell."

Chapter 6

The Paradox of the Cross

After having discussed the mystery of suffering from the biblical perspective, I explored how suffering was at the very center of the Christian life in the Middle Ages. In the face of pain and suffering, there was a call to identify with the suffering Lord. The twentieth century experienced some social, political, and economic improvements. However, there remained many challenges as the world faced the two major world wars. For Schillebeeckx (1914–2009) and Marthe Robin (1902–1986), two contemporaries of the twentieth century, their Christian understanding of the mystery of the cross widely diverged. Marthe Robin, who lived in France, believed that pain and suffering was an opportunity to identify with the suffering Lord, as St. Paul urges us to do in Colossians 1:24. She similarly understood her plight, but also believed that she was made a victim of God. And she learned through her suffering to love God and the neighbor. Schillebeeckx saw and understood suffering in the world as incompatible, incongruous with God's revelation in the scriptures, but most importantly with God's self-communication in the ministry of the Son. For him, the mystery of suffering reveals nothing but God's presence on the side of suffering humanity. Why are these two contemporaries so different in their understanding of the mystery of suffering? What do they have in common, and what differentiates them?

6.1. Two Different Worlds in the Same World

It is essential to start by repeating what we already said in the previous chapters about these two people, namely, Marthe Robin and Edward Schillebeeckx. Schillebeeckx was a theologian. While he spent most of his adult life in the academy, he claimed that his theology was not primarily for the elite, but for the ordinary people. It may not be off the mark to presume that Schillebeeckx was writing and doing theology for people like Marthe Robin.

As already mentioned, Marthe Robin was barely educated. She could not even finish her elementary school because of her sickly nature. Unlike Schillebeeckx, she did not belong to the elite, did not know much theology. While it is believed that Marthe read or had people read to her, she most likely would have been much more conversant with popular spiritualities, or the spiritual practices of her time. If we take seriously, as mentioned in chapter 5, the fact that Chateau de Galore in "the Plains" of France at the time of Marthe was not a place of extraordinary faith, one can also infer that her religious practice, like her people's, was minimal.

If Schillebeeckx claims, as I pointed out in the fourth chapter, that he was writing primarily but not exclusively for ordinary Christians like Marthe Robin, how is it that his orientation on suffering seemed so different from hers? Both of them saw, and experienced, even if from a distance, the atrocities of the Second World War and the concentration camps. But how is it that they interpret suffering differently?

6.2. Academic Theologian versus a Mystic

We cannot deny that during the ninety-five living years of Schillebeeckx, he, from time to time, fell sick, tired, and unwell. He might have felt the pain of people suffering around him. But we have no evidence that Schillebeeckx went through suffering and pain for a long period of time. He did his theology, it seems to me, from the comfort of his armchair as he observed and analyzed the abundance of sufferings and pain around him. Nagasaki, Hiroshima, Buchenwald, Auschwitz, and Vietnam were vivid realities on the minds of people. These realities were so atrocious that it seemed almost impossible, almost inhumane, for someone to look at a survivor in the face and justify what s/he has gone through. How do you tell a direct survivor of Buchenwald or Auschwitz that what s/he has just gone through is the will of God, or the punishment for sins, or an opportunity to share in the suffering of Christ? How could one religiously justify such outrageously evil actions? For Schillebeeckx, who did theology from his vantage point as an academic, it was much easier to blame humanity. Human beings are sinful, and their wounded freedom leads to decisions that make them or others suffer. This concept was well-known. The scriptures maintained it, Saints Augustine and Thomas Aquinas held on to it as well. The only problem, though, is that Schillebeeckx did not make the slightest room for God's responsibility in human suffering. "God is pure positivity," he claims, "we cannot look for the ground of suffering in God," he continues. And he ends his argument by radically suggesting that "the cross is the index of the anti-divine." He uses neither the language of permissibility nor allowance, though he does affirm that by creating human beings who have freedom, God has made himself vulnerable to their decisions and actions.[359] For him, evil, suffering, and pain are antithetical to God, who is pure positivity. But how can we put the weight of such a massive evil and the death of the Son of God only on the conscience of humanity? How do we, in the face of an all-powerful and just God, blame only humanity for the atrocities committed at Nagasaki, Hiroshima, Buchenwald, Auschwitz, or Vietnam? Where was God when humankind was misbehaving?

Marthe Robin spoke and wrote about something that she was personally experiencing. Suffering and pain were not strange to Marthe. From the age of three months to her death in 1981 at the age of seventy-nine, she lived through suffering and pain. She felt the pain of the death of family members, fragile health, being paralyzed, and having to be confined to one place, thirst and hunger, and more importantly the stigmata. When she spoke about suffering, she was living it in her flesh. Strangely enough, Marthe Robin didn't directly blame human beings for her plight. In fact, I do not think she could have accused anyone. For even though Marthe remained sick her

[359] Cf. Edward Schillebeeckx, Church: The Human Story of God, trans. John Bowden (NY: Crossroad, 1993), 90.

entire life, family members, friends, and relatives were quite often kind to her. Consequently, she turned to God whom she claims had made her his victim, but to whom she was grateful. According to Bernard Peyrous,

> She was full of gratitude to God for granting her the grace of being so close to him as to share in his Passion. On Wednesday 9 January 1935, she wrote: "Each day I embrace with renewed gratitude and renewed joy the immense task entrusted to me by the Redeemer and thank him for having so prodigiously given me of his chalice, his crown, his nails and his holy cross, for having granted that *I might experience and continue his long and painful agony and all his Passion*, for having in short so prodigiously and profoundly imprinted in me his suffering and Eucharistic life."[360]

Marthe seemed to have come to believe that through her suffering, she was continuing the Passion of Christ. In a sense, being united to Jesus, she was suffering like he did for the salvation of souls. We can once again recall her saying, "I am covered with blood... but I ardently accept the prolongation of my pilgrimage... I have only one desire: to save the souls by loving God more and more." And before that, she wrote to her friend Sister Marie-Thérèse, asking her to pray for her so that she "may learn to suffer for the salvation of souls, to suffer so that Jesus may be loved." Can one decide that his/her suffering, in whatever form, is for the salvation of souls? Schillebeeckx explained that while the Father never wished the death of the Son for the reparation of sins, the Son was able, thanks to God's grace, to incorporate in his death the salvation of humanity. Schillebeeckx may not have been the first to have made this assumption. The author of the Letter to the Hebrews seemed to have sug-

---

[360] Bernard Peyrous, Marthe Robin: A Prophetic Vision of the Gospel Message, loc. 921–925, with added emphasis.

gested the same. He writes, "In the days of his flesh, Jesus offered up prayers and supplications, with loud cries and tears, to him who was able to save him from death, and he was heard because of his reverence" (Hebrews 5:7). While Jesus still suffered and died, the author of Hebrews maintains that he was heard, because thanks to God's grace, Jesus's desire to incorporate in his death the intention of carrying upon himself our sins for the salvation of humanity was heard. Moreover, God vindicated his death by bringing him back to life (the resurrection). Was Marthe's prayer to suffer for the salvation of the souls similar to Jesus'? Could it be that Marthe also carried upon herself the sins of humanity and suffered for the salvation of humankind? Raymond Peyret explains that after the stigmata, multiple times during her weekly (every Thursday to Friday night) passion, Marthe was like Christ. "Like Christ at Gethsemane, she carried the sins of the world. She was overwhelmed and horrified; she *became* sin. Sometimes she would say to Fr. Fine, 'Do not come near me! I will make you dirty!' She groaned, unable to say any more."[361] I believe this is an interpretation that Raymond Peyret gives to the suffering and expressions of Marthe.

For Marthe, it seems to me, the love of God and neighbor was that which was at the center of her entire experience. In service to the love of God, she was ready for all that came her way, for that love to be revealed to humanity, thus attracting her beloved brothers and sisters to God. Bernard Peyrous clarifies this when he says,

> She was not going through this for her own sake. There are references in her writings to those she loves and to causes dear to her, especially the holiness of priests: "Ah!" she said, "I would so like to show everyone the Christ full of love and mercy, in order to draw them to God." [and he explains:] Marthe was becoming more and more conscious of her intercessory role. She held in her

---

[361] Raymond Peyret, Marthe Robin: The Cross and the Joy, 55.

prayers the souls she knew, but in this respect too she was expanding her horizons.[362]

Sometime on February 2, 1930, just some few months before the stigmata, she is remembered to have written,

"May God make me a foyer to purify the world and set souls ablaze." Later, on 14 May 1934, [after she received the stigmata] she noted that God had told her: "I have chosen you to rekindle the love that is dying out in the world, to serve as my helper and reveal my Work. I shall make you a flame of the fire that I wish to light on the earth." On 22 January 1936, there is another quite similar passage written by her: "It seems to be my mission to spread the reign of truth and love over the earth. I believe I have said it many times, but I can't help saying it again: all I want to leave behind as a trace of my passing here below is an immense light of truth and a great fire of divine love. I would like people to love one another as I love them."[363]

Maybe in these cases humanity indirectly has something to do with her suffering, which she maintains comes from God who made her his victim. Marthe, however, accepted everything out of love and in love, as she prayed for the grace that her suffering may be for the salvation of souls, just as Jesus's was.

---

[362] Bernard Peyrous, Marthe Robin: A Prophetic Vision of the Gospel Message, loc. 930–935.
[363] Ibid, loc. 1074–1078.

6.3. The Paradox of the Cross

Throughout his theological writings, Schillebeeckx insisted that God did not put Jesus on the cross. He maintained this for the multiple reasons that we have already referenced. If God did not put his Son on the cross, for what reason does his Son put others (the stigmatics) on the cross? "Do you wish to be like me?" Jesus asked Marthe before giving her the stigmata. If the Triune God is thus pure positivity and does in no case will the suffering of humanity, how do we explain that Jesus, the Son of God, God, is directly, at least according to Marthe Robin's experience and account of the events, responsible for her painful stigmata? While one could make room for humanity's finitude—that is, the limited lifespan of fleshy creature—in understanding the health troubles of Marthe, for Schillebeeckx, it would be absurd to think that the God of love ever inflicts his beloved servants with pains and sufferings of what he never wished for his Son: the cross.

Consequently, the question is, how do we prove Jesus indeed did this to Marthe? Well, no one will ever be able to determine that. She was the only one that had the vision and knew what happened that day. Besides, we only have her interpretation of her experience. However, Marthe is not the only mystic that went through these troubling events of Jesus inflicting the marks of the stigmata. We know St. Francis, Padre Pio, Therese Neumann, et al., whose stigmata appeared after an intense encounter with the divine. It is unequivocally clear that strong faith and trust in Jesus are at the foundation of the extraordinary religious experience that precedes the appearance of stigmata. As Jean Barbier writes, "Les stigmatisés sont une réponse [...] ils nous rappellent la vivante présence de Dieu."[364] According to Barbier, there is no doubt God is responsible for such brutal and

---

[364] Jean Barbier, Trois Stigmatisés: Thérèse Neumann, Le Padre Pio, Marthe Robin (Paris: Téqui, 1987), 7. The translation which is mine is, "Stigmatics are a response,…they remind us of the real presence of God."

suffering pains that the stigmatics go through. Raymond Peyret on the same issue writes,

> To few of his privileged followers, God has given the gift of experiencing the very suffering of Christ in their own bodies. This was the case, for example, with Francis of Assisi, Catherine of Siena, and in our century, with Theresa Neumann and Marthe Robin. "I cannot conceive of Love," said Charles de Foucauld, "unaccompanied by the most pressing need to imitate." "Do you wish to be like me?" Jesus asked Marthe Robin. Marthe was not content to contemplate the crucified Christ. She suffered with him and shared his Passion.[365]

For Barbier and Peyret, maybe God, indeed, does store up pain and suffering for his children (Cf. Job 21:19). For it is God who inflicts pain on the stigmatics, considered his privileged followers, as a reminder that he is still present and active in the world, or as a way of configuring these (stigmatics) to his Son. Will Barbier agree that the cross, the once-and-for-all suffering (Roman 6:10) of the Son more than two thousand years ago, was an act of God's manifestation of his active presence in the world? Would Schillebeeckx accept that the pains and suffering of the cross, never willed by God for his Son, but now inflicted on the stigmatics are the sign of the Lord's active manifestation in the world? Did God's positivity and hatred for evil, pain, and suffering end with the death of his Son so much so that now he can tolerate suffering as a sign of his presence among us? Do stigmatics have to become victims of the pains and the suffering of the crucified Lord for us to know that God does exist? Are the stigmata the only way to be like Jesus? I do not have definite answers to these questions. However, if the mystics' experience is real and God is the one that gives them these sufferings and painful stigmata, then

---

[365] Raymond Peyret, Marthe Robin: The Cross and the Joy, 57.

evil and pain can no longer be merely the mark of the anti-divine in the world.

The most interesting element, however, it seems to me, is that despite the pain and suffering that the stigmatics go through, they seem to have a certain consolation. A power that allows them to sail through the suffering with much optimism. Marthe Robin, after receiving the stigmata, is remembered, on December 31, 1930, to have said,

> My whole being has undergone a transforma-
> tion as mysterious as it is profound. A year of
> trials, a year of pain. A year of graces and of love.
> My real joy on my sickbed is profound, lasting
> because divine… I reflect upon the road I have
> traveled since the beginning of my illness, and
> from this reflection emerges only Love, and
> gratitude towards God who is so merciful and
> so good. What a labor! What growth God has
> wrought in me! But what leaping of the heart,
> what death-struggles of the will it takes to die to
> self![366]

Marthe seems to suggest that her sickness was pain and trial, but once God gave her the marks of the crucified Lord, there was a transformation. Raymond Peyret refers to Marthe's transformation as the crossing of a new threshold in her life.[367] For she then sees and realizes God's merciful love and care. Bernard Peyrous notes,

> She was having the greatest possible experience
> any human being can have: that of feeling God
> living within her. On 26 January 1932, she wrote:
> "Never before have I been in a state of such com-
> plete transformation into the adorable suffering

---

[366] Ibid, 54.

[367] Cf. Raymond Peyret, Marthe Robin: The Cross and the Joy, 54.

and loving humanity of Jesus. Of Jesus, assimilating, absorbing, exhausting, melting my whole being in him… New life in a surfeit of self-abandonment and love! More than ever given up to the transforming action of the Holy Spirit… To Jesus, to Christ—the Host, in order to conform to his image and be in his likeness."[368]

As mysterious as this may sound, the agony of the passion brings trust and faith in a loving God—a God who comes around in love to save. In this case, salvation is not understood in terms of God saving from pain and suffering, but in terms of the suffering Lord absorbing into himself the suffering stigmatic. Such an experience of complete identification with Jesus leads the sigmatic to radically entrust himself/herself to the love and care of the Father who remains present whenever the Son suffers. Generally speaking, the overarching reaction of stigmatics is that they feel their suffering is nothing compared to the presence and the love of God which they experience during the times of Gethsemane and Golgotha. This is where Schillebeeckx's and Marthe Robin's theologies of suffering meet.

Schillebeeckx understands that Jesus's reference to Psalm 22 during his passion is a mark of his trust in his *Abba*[369] who became exceptionally close and present to him. He explains, "The entire Golgotha event is interpreted—or rather perceived—in terms of Psalm 22."[370] However, he is also aware that some, like Jürgen Moltmann, have interpreted Jesus's cry of distress ("My God, my God, why have you forsaken me" [Psalm 22:1]) on the cross as a sign

---

[368] Bernard Peyrous, Marthe Robin: A Prophetic Vision of the Gospel Message, loc. 925–930.

[369] Schillebeeckx explains that "Jesus' Abba experience is that his unique turning to the Father is 'preceded' in absolute priority and is inwardly supported by the Father's unique turning to Jesus. Early Christian tradition calls this self-communication of the Father—ground, and source of Jesus' Abba experience—the Word." See Edward Schillebeeckx, The Collected Works of Edward Schillebeeckx Volume 6: Jesus: An Experiment in Christology, loc. 15731.

[370] Edward Schillebeeckx, The Collected Works of Edward Schillebeeckx Volume 6: Jesus: An Experiment in Christology, loc. 6824.

of the Father's abandonment of the Son. Such an interpretation of Jesus's prayer or quotation of Psalm 22:1 on the cross is quite misleading and lacks any scriptural basis. Shillebeeckx suggests,

> [A]part from the uncertainty whether this quotation of the psalm goes back to the historical Jesus or to a later Christian interpretation, in Jewish spirituality the quotation of the beginning of a psalm (no matter by whom) was an evocation, a reminder of the whole psalm. Now the basic mood of Psalm 22 emerges from a great many verses: "for he has not despised or abhorred the affliction of the afflicted; and has not hidden his face from him, but has heard, when he cries to him" (Psalm 22:24); and "All the ends of the earth shall remember and turn to the Lord" (Psalm 22:27); and finally, "Before him shall bow all who go down to the dust, and he who cannot keep himself alive" (Psalm 22:29b). This psalm therefore expresses the believer's conviction that in situations where God's redemptive help and support cannot actually be experienced, in situations in which men no longer experience any glimmer of hope, in impossible situations, *God nevertheless remains near at hand* and that salvation consists in the fact that man still holds fast to God's invisible hand *in* this dark night of faith.[371]

Ryan explains, "According to Schillebeeckx's interpretation of the crucifixion, God does not intervene to save Jesus or to remove the starkness of death, but neither does God abandon Jesus. Jesus did not receive any favored treatment from God whom he enjoyed a unique relationship. [...] God is silently present to Jesus at this moment,

---

[371] Edward Schillebeeckx, Christ, the Experience of Jesus as Lord, 824–825.

just as God is silently present to all those who suffer."[372] The paradox is that while pain and suffering remain antithetical to God, he stayed present and very close to the Son. The manifestation of God's hidden presence during the passion is revealed at the resurrection of Christ.[373]

Taking the cue from Schillebeeckx's intuition about Psalm 22 as prayed by Jesus in Matthew 27:46 and Mark 15:34, I am tempted to ask, "Could it be that the stigmata are the only way through which God could get as close as he could ever be to Marthe Robin? Could it be that the stigmata of Marthe were God's way of granting her prayers of offering her suffering for the salvation of souls?" Schillebeeckx may say "yes" with a "but." Yes, for he stipulates, "To put one's trust in Jesus is to ground oneself in the ground of his experience: the Father. It implies acknowledging the authentic, non-illusory reality of Jesus' *Abba* experience."[374] This is the same experience that allowed Jesus to feel and know the proximity of his Father, whose loving redemption he could trust in as he hung on the cross. In that same experience of his *Abba* granting grace, Jesus knew that his death was redemptive. It consequently seems that, by offering a chance to the mystic, through the stigmata, to be in intense solidarity with the suffering Lord, Jesus allows her to become him, in his *Abba* experience. The Father sees the mystic, who puts her trust in Jesus, as he saw the Son more than two thousand years ago and gets the closest to her he can ever be. As the mystic suffers, the Father is present and very close and makes her suffering redemptive.

But if it is true that God does inflict pain and suffering as his way of getting the closest he can ever be, and transforming suffering into redemptive suffering, then what does that say about his pure positivity, the cross being the index of the anti-divine, and his place in the origin or cause of evil? For even though the stigmata, in this case of Marthe Robin, seem to exonerate God—because they represent for her the time the Lord came the closest and took control of

---

[372] Robin Ryan, God and the Mystery of Human Suffering, 229–230.

[373] Cf. Edward Schillebeeckx, Christ, the Experience of Jesus as Lord, 825.

[374] Edward Schillebeeckx, The Collected Works of Edward Schillebeeckx Volume 6: Jesus: An Experiment in Christology, loc. 15325–15328.

her frail health—the pain and suffering that go with them do not acquit him. The suggestion here is that we cannot just understand the cross as the index of the anti-divine, or merely absolve God from any responsibility from suffering and pain.

Marthe Robin went through a lot of pain and suffering. In her words, through her pain and suffering, she was the "little victim of Jesus." Her pain, culminated in the stigmata (the cross), was the index of the divine. As for the devil, we know he appeared only in three different instances. He, first, broke her teeth, then made her extremely thirsty when she could neither eat nor drink and, finally, attacked her during her weekly passions. Therefore, we cannot accuse him for all the misfortunes in Marthe's life. God's place is quite significant. Leaving aside the other suffering—including those she faced after her full consecration to God—God is the one who unequivocally afflicts Marthe Robin with the painful and suffering marks of the crucified Lord; God, according to her interpretation of her experience, gave her the cross. While I could blame God for preparing her to accept the stigmata through her initial suffering, I do not, because there is no such evidence for that. If I conjecture that closeness to the sufferer and transformation of the sufferer's initial pain are the reasons for the stigmata, a question will remain about Schillebeeckx's claim of the cross being the index of the anti-divine and God's pure positivity. Another question will be raised about those mystics who were not particularly sick or suffering but did receive the stigmata. Schillebeeckx's message of Jesus being a bringer of God's radical "no" to the continuing history of human suffering[375] seems very challenging in relation to Marthe Robin and the many other stigmatic mystics. From the theology of Schillebeeckx and the mystical experience of Marthe Robin, in the face of pain and suffering, we can at least take consolation in the fact that God is always present, and he is the closest he can ever be.

---

[375] / Cf. Edward Schillebeeckx, The Collected Works of Edward Schillebeeckx Volume 6: Jesus: An Experiment in Christology, loc. 3927.

6.4. A Pastoral Response to the Origin of Suffering

The presence of God to the sufferer is very vital and essential. While the effort to decipher and explicitly communicate the origin of suffering may be a very complicated one, it is not difficult to demonstrate God's radical presence when humanity suffers. Whether God allows evil, is at its origin, or opposes it, in all cases, the Lord seems always to be present when people suffer. This is the overall religious reaction, expressed by Marthe and Schillebeeckx, to the mystery of suffering. Even though Marthe Robin believed in her heart that her pain and suffering was an opportunity offered to her by the suffering Lord, there is absolutely no evidence that she ever thought God had deserted her. Schillebeeckx, who maintains that the cross is the index of the anti-divine, also forcefully suggests the closeness of God, to his suffering Son Jesus, and consequently, today to suffering humanity.

When humanity suffers, our quest should not be who is responsible; it should preferably be an affirmation of God's presence. "Maybe God does not cause our suffering. Maybe it happens for some reason other than the will of God. The psalmist writes, 'I lift up my eyes to the hills; from where does my help come? My help comes from the Lord, maker of the Heaven and earth' [Psalm 121:1–2]. He does not say, 'My pain comes from the Lord,' or, 'my tragedy comes from the Lord.' He says, 'My *help* comes from the Lord.'"[376] However, if there is need to affirm the origin of the sufferer's suffering, that responsibility rests squarely on him/her. If the one going through suffering and pain for some reasons known to him/her alone understands his/her plight as coming from God, so be it. But if for a similar reason the one going through the troubles of life seems to believe that God did allow that to happen to him/her, so be it as well. And finally, if someone thinks that God did neither enable nor cause his/her pain and suffering and attributes it to some other realities, that experience should not be dismissed either. The most important thing for a listening and compassionate pastoral agent is to understand the experi-

---

[376] Harold S. Kushner, When Bad Things Happen to Good People, Reprint edition (NY: Anchor, 2004), 35.

ence of the one suffering and always to reaffirm God's presence in all circumstances. For the origin or circumstances of pain and suffering in the world do not make any statement on the love, justice, power, and goodness of God. To me, it seems, it is our collective reaction to suffering and pain in the world that affirms or not the nature of God. A collective response that entirely excludes God from the picture is most likely a hindrance. Pope Francis, in the context of holiness, recently wrote,

> We should not grow discouraged before examples of holiness that appear unattainable. There are some testimonies that may prove helpful and inspiring, but that we are not meant to copy, for that could even lead us astray from the one specific path that the Lord has in mind for us. The important thing is that each believer discern his or her own path, that they bring out the very best of themselves, the most personal gifts that God has placed in their hearts (cf. 1 Cor 12:7), rather than hopelessly trying to imitate something not meant for them. We are all called to be witnesses, but there are many actual ways of bearing witness. Indeed, when the great mystic, Saint John of the Cross, wrote his Spiritual Canticle, he preferred to avoid hard and fast rules for all. He explained that his verses were composed so that everyone could benefit from them "in his or her own way." For God's life is communicated "to some in one way and to others in another."[377]

Not everyone can bear witness to God by accepting suffering as coming from the suffering Lord as Marthe Robin did. And it is not

---

[377] Pope Francis, Gaudete et Exsultate: Apostolic Exhortation on the Call to Holiness in Today's World, (2018) no. 11, http://w2.vatican.va/content/francesco/en/apost_exhortations/documents/papa-francesco_esortazione-ap_20180319_gaudete-et-exsultate.html.

everyone who can believe and take God's innocence for granted—as Schillebeeckx considered—when they face suffering. But in one way or another, most people will be comforted and keenly captivated in knowing that God is ever-present.

Bibliography

Barbier, Jean. *Trois Stigmatisés: Thérèse Neumann, Le Padre Pio, Marthe Robin.* Paris: Téqui, 1987.

Bellitto, Christopher M. *Ten Ways the Church Has Changed: What History Can Teach Us about Uncertain Times.* Boston, MA: Pauline Books & Media, 2006.

Biot, René. *The Enigma of the Stigmata.* 1st ed. NY: Hawthorn Books, 1962.

Crossan, John Dominic. *Who Killed Jesus? Exposing the Roots of Anti-Semitism in the Gospel Story of the Death of Jesus.* 1st ed. SF: HarperSanFrancisco, 1995.

"Christ's Descension into Hades to Destroy Death." http://classical-christianity.com/2011/04/23/christs-descension-into-hades-to-destroy-death/. Accessed on April 6, 2018.

Dealy, Ross. *The Stoic Origins of Erasmus' Philosophy of Christ.* 1st edition. Toronto; Buffalo; London: University of Toronto Press, Scholarly Publishing Division, 2017.

Dupuis, Jacques. *Who Do You Say I Am? Introduction to Christology.* Maryknoll, NY: Orbis, 1994.

Elledge, Casey Deryl, and C. D. Elledge. *Resurrection of the Dead in Early Judaism, 200 BCE–CE 200.* Oxford University Press, 2017.

Foley, Daniel Patrick. "Eleven Interpretations of Personal Suffering." *Journal of Religion and Health* 27, no. 4 (1988): 321–28.

Freze, Michael. *They Bore the Wounds of Christ: The Mystery of the Sacred Stigmata.* Huntington, Ind.: Our Sunday Visitor, 1989.

Galvin John P. "Retelling the Story of Jesus: Christology." In *The Praxis of Christian Experience: An Introduction to the Theology of Edward Schillebeeckx.* eds. Robert J. Schreiter, and Mary Catherine Hilkert. 1st ed. 52–67. SF: Harpercollins, 1989.

Harrington, Daniel J. *Why Do We Suffer? A Scriptural Approach to the Human Condition*. Franklin, Wis.: Sheed & Ward, 2000.

Hill, William J. "Human Happiness as God's Honor: Background to a Theology in Transition." In *The Praxis of Christian Experience: An Introduction to the Theology of Edward Schillebeeckx*. eds. Robert J. Schreiter, and Mary Catherine Hilkert. 1st ed. 1–17. SF: Harpercollins, 1989.

Hilkert, Mary Catherine. "The Discovery of the Living God: Revelation and Experience." In *The Praxis of Christian Experience: An Introduction to the Theology of Edward Schillebeeckx*. eds. Robert J. Schreiter, and Mary Catherine Hilkert. 1st ed. 35–51. SF: Harpercollins, 1989.

Kushner, Harold S. *When Bad Things Happen to Good People*. Knopf Doubleday Publishing Group, 2007.

Lambrecht, Jan. *Second Corinthians*. Collegeville, Minn.: Liturgical Press, 1999.

Metz, Johann Baptist. "Suffering unto God." Trans. J. Matthew Ashley, *Critical Inquiry* 20, no. 4 (1994): 611–22.

Miller, Richard B. "Evil, Friendship, and Iconic Realism in Augustine's 'Confessions.'" *The Harvard Theological Review* 104, no. 4 (2011): 387–409.

O'Collins, Gerald. "What Are They Saying about Jesus Now?" *The Furrow*, 1981, 203–211.

Peyret, Raymond. *Marthe Robin: The Cross and the Joy*. NY: Alba House, 1983.

Peyrous, Bernard. *Marthe Robin: A Prophetic Vision of the Gospel Message*. Trans. Kathryn Spink. Dublin: Veritas Publications, 2010.

Pope Benedict XVI. *Jesus of Nazareth: From the Baptism in the Jordan to the Transfiguration*. 1st edition. NY: Doubleday, 2007.

Pope Francis. *Gaudete et Exsultate: Apostolic Exhortation on the Call to Holiness in Today's World*. http://w2.vatican.va/content/francesco/en/apost_exhortations/documents/papa-francesco_esortazione-ap_20180319_gaudete-et-exsultate.html. Accessed May 3, 2018.

Portier, William L. "Interpretation and Method." In *The Praxis of Christian Experience: An Introduction to the Theology of Edward Schillebeeckx*. eds. Robert J. Schreiter, and Mary Catherine Hilkert. 1st ed. 18–34. SF: Harpercollins, 1989.

Roest Bert. "A Meditative Spectacle: Christ's Bodily Passion in the Satirica Ystoria." In *The Broken Body: Passion Devotion in Late-Medieval Culture*. eds. Schlusemann, R. M., Bernhard. Ridderbos, and A. A. MacDonald. Mediaevalia Groningana, no. 21. 31–54. Groningen: Egbert Forsten, 1998.

Ross, Ellen M. *The Grief of God: Images of the Suffering Jesus in Late Medieval England*. NY: Oxford University Press, 1997.

Ross Susan M. "Salvation in and for the World: Church and Sacraments." In *The Praxis of Christian Experience: An Introduction to the Theology of Edward Schillebeeckx*. eds. Robert J. Schreiter, and Mary Catherine Hilkert. 1st ed. 101–115. SF: Harpercollins, 1989.

Ryan, Robin. *God and the Mystery of Human Suffering: A Theological Conversation Across the Ages*. NY: Paulist Press, 2011.

———. "Holding on to the Hand of God: Edward Schillebeeckx on the Mystery of Suffering." *New Blackfriars* 89, no. 1019 (January 2008): 114–25.

———. *Jesus and Salvation: Soundings in the Christian Tradition and Contemporary Theology*. Collegeville, Minnesota: Liturgical Press, 2015.

Saint Augustine. *On the Trinity*. ed. by Philip Schaff, n.d. 1887.

Schillebeeckx, Edward. *Christ, the Experience of Jesus as Lord*. NY: Seabury Press, 1980.

———. *Church: The Human Story of God*. Translated by John Bowden. NY: Crossroad, 1993.

———. *God among Us: The Gospel Proclaimed*. NY: Crossroad Pub., 1983.

———. *The Collected Works of Edward Schillebeeckx Volume 6: Jesus: An Experiment in Christology*. Kindle edition. London: T&T Clark, 2014.

Senior, Donald. *The Passion of Jesus in the Gospel of John*. Collegeville, Minn.: Liturgical Press, 1991.

————. *The Passion of Jesus in the Gospel of Luke*. Wilmington, Del.: M. Glazier, 1989.

————. *The Passion of Jesus in the Gospel of Mark*. Wilmington, Del.: M. Glazier, 1984.

————. *The Passion of Jesus in the Gospel of Matthew*. Wilmington, Del.: M. Glazier, 1985.

————. *Why the Cross?* Nashville: Abingdon Press, 2014.

Shinners, John Raymond, ed. *Medieval Popular Religion, 1000–1500: A Reader*. Readings in Medieval Civilizations and Cultures 2. Peterborough, Ont., Canada; Orchard Park, NY: Broadview Press, 1997.

Sobrino, Jon. *Christ the Liberator: A View from the Victims*. 9/22/01 edition. Maryknoll, NY: Orbis Books, 2001.

Swanson R. N. "Passion and Practice: The Social and Ecclesiastical Implications of the Passion Devotion in the Late Middle Ages." In *The Broken Body: Passion Devotion in Late-Medieval Culture*. eds. Schlusemann, R. M., Bernhard. Ridderbos, and A. A. MacDonald. Mediaevalia Groningana, no. 21. 1–30. Groningen: Egbert Forsten, 1998.

Stark, Thom, and John J. Collins. *The Human Faces of God: What Scripture Reveals When It Gets God Wrong*. 1st edition. Eugene, Or: Wipf & Stock Pub, 2011.

Still, Todd D. "The Vocation to Participate in Christ's Suffering." In *Suffering in Romans*, edited by Siu Fung Wu, 98–129. James Clarke & Co Ltd, 2015.

Thiel, John E. *God, Evil, and Innocent Suffering: A Theological Reflection*. NY: Crossroad, 2002.

Webster, John B. "Edward Schillebeeckx: God Is 'Always Absolutely New.'" *Evangel: A Quarterly Review of Biblical, Practical and Contemporary Theology 2*, no. 4, (1984): 5–10.

Wilson, Ian. *Stigmata: An Investigation into the Mysterious Appearance of Christ's Wounds in Hundreds of People from Medieval Italy to Modern America*. 1st U.S. ed. San Francisco: Harper & Row, 1989.

Appendix 1

Act of Abandonment to the Love and the Will of God

"Lord, My God, you have asked everything of your little servant; take and receive everything, then. This day I belong to you without any reservation, forever. O Beloved of my soul! It is you only whom I want, and for your love I renounce all.

"O God of Love! Take my memory and all its memories, take my intelligence so that it will act only for your greater glory; take my will entirely, so that it will forever be drowned in your own; never again what I want O most sweet Jesus, but always what you want; receive me, guide me, sanctify me, direct me; to abandon myself.

"O God of all goodness, take my body and all its senses, my spirit and all its faculties, my heart and all its affections; O adorable Savior, you are the sole owner of my soul and of all my being; receive the immolation, that every day and every hour, I offer you in silence; deign accept it and change it into graces and blessings for all those I love, for the conversion of sinners, and for the sanctification of souls.

"O Jesus! Take all of my little heart; it begs and sighs to belong to you alone; hold it always in your powerful hand so that it will surrender and pour itself out to no other creature.

"Lord, take and sanctify all my words, all my actions, all my desires. Be for my soul its good and its all. To you I give and abandon it.

"I accept with love all that you send me: pain, sorrow, Joy, consolation, dryness, shame, desertion, scorn, humiliation, work, suffering, trials, everything that comes to me from you, everything that you wish, O Jesus.

"I submit humbly to the glorious control of your providence in supporting me solely by the help of your immense goodness; I promise you the most sincere fidelity. O Divine Savior, as a victim for the salvation of souls, I surrender and abandon myself to you.

"I implore you to accept all of my offering, I and I will then be happy and trusting. Alas! It is all too little, I know, but I haven't anything else; I love my extreme worthlessness, because it will abstain for me your mercy and all your paternal solicitude.

"My God you know my frailty and the bottomless abyss of my weakness. If, one day, I were to be unfaithful to your sovereign will, if I were to recoil before suffering and the cross, and to stray from your path of love, fleeing the tender protection of your arms, oh! I beg and implore you for the grace of dying at that instant. Pardon me, O Sacred Heart of my Savior, forgive me by your most sweet name of Jesus, by the sorrows of Mary, by the intercession of Saint Joseph, and by the Love that you had in doing your Father's Will.

"O God my soul! O Divine Sun! I love you, I bless you, I praise you, I abandon myself completely to you. I take refuge in you; hide me in your bosom, for my being shudders under the burden of the cruel afflictions that crush me on all sides—and I am always alone.

"My Beloved, help me, take me with you. In you alone I wish to live so that in you alone I may die."

About the Author

Augustin Kassa, SMA, was born in 1981 in the small French-speaking country of Togo on the West African coast. After his elementary, middle, and high school in his home country, he joined the Society of African Missions (SMA) in 2004. Upon becoming a temporary member of the SMA in June 2007, he became a permanent member in May 2011 and was ordained a Catholic priest in July 2012.

After being admitted to the SMA in 2004, he was sent to Nigeria to study philosophy. Then he went to the Benin Republic for the spiritual year. He spent his field training year (2007–2008) in Zambia, in the Diocese of Ndola, where he worked mostly with the youth.

His years of theological formation took place in Nairobi (2008–2012) in Tangaza College, where he graduated with a sacred theology baccalaureate (STB). While he studied theology, he also developed a great interest in youth ministry that he studied. After his ordination, he was assigned to Accra, Ghana, where he worked in a parish, but also with the Youth of Madina Vicariate. Two years later, he was reassigned to the USA and, since then, has been working in the Diocese of Peoria. In fall 2015, he got admission at the Catholic Theological Union (CTU) in Chicago, Illinois, from where he recently graduated with a master's of art in systematic theology.